113 things to do by 13

P9-CAA-176

113 things to do by 13

with tips from your fave celebs and tween insiders

brittany macleod

with a little help from mom, *Access Hollywood*'s Terri MacLeod

HARLEQUIN®

A Stonesong Press Book

HARLEQUIN

ISBN-13: 978-0-373-89212-9
ISBN-10:   0-373-89212-8

Copyright © 2009 by The Stonesong Press, LLC and Terri MacLeod

A Stonesong Press Book

113 Things to do by 13

For information, address Harlequin.
Harlequin Enterprises Ltd.
225 Duncan Mill Rd. Don Mills,
Ontario M3B 3K9

FIRST EDITION

LIBRARY OF CONGRESS CATALOGING-IN-PUBLICATION DATA
MacLeod, Brittany.
 113 things to do by 13 : with tips from your fave celebs and tween insiders
/ Brittany MacLeod, with a little help from mom, Terri MacLeod. --
1st ed.
  p. cm. -- (A Stonesong Press book)
ISBN 978-0-373-89212-9 (pbk.)
1. Games for girls--Juvenile literature. 2. Amusements--Juvenile literature.
I. MacLeod, Terri. II. Title. III. Title: One hundred thirteen things to do by 13.

GV1204.998.M32 2008

790.1'94--dc22

                    2008053710

10 9 8 7 6 5 4 3 2 1

Designed by Georgia Rucker Design

dedication

Grandma & Papa MacLeod

&

Tweenagers Everywhere

introduction

People talk a lot about how tough it is to be a teenager. But what about being a tWeeNager?... Talk about **drama**! Just cuz we're not dealing with college apps or major boy issues yet, doesn't mean serious stuff isn't happening in our lives. We've got **crazy/busy** schedules, our bodies keep changing, our best buds are acting weird, our parents are bugging—and we're **stressing** from all the pressure to be and do a lot of different things (some of which are impossible, like getting the mean girl to hike it to another school or dating a JoNas Brother!)

I hope this book will help young girls everywhere transition into their teenage years with a positive attitude, tons of **girl power**, and the inspiration to be and appreciate yourself for simply **BEING YOU!** (Remember: it's cool to be different.) I like to think of 113 Things To Do By 13 as the go-to guide to being a hip n' happening n' totally competeNt tWeeNager! More than 100 peeps contributed their expertise and packed the following pages with tips on everything from the coolest fashion musts to DIy crafts to smart-girl advice on **gossip**, cyber-bullying, **crushes**, body issues, and making *big dreams* happen at a young age. Even a few of our fave celebs, like Selena Gomez and the Camp Rock gals, shared their teen **survival** tips.

So, jump to your favorite section or read it cover-to-cover! May you enjoy reading *113 Things To Do By 13*, as much as I liked writing it and discovering for myself why 13 is such an awesome age. Hey, there's **plenty of time** (at least a few years) to stress about getting our license, college, and not to mention that...

work thing. So, let's kick off our teen years in a **super fab** way— and celebrate all the great things we can do and learn right *now*.

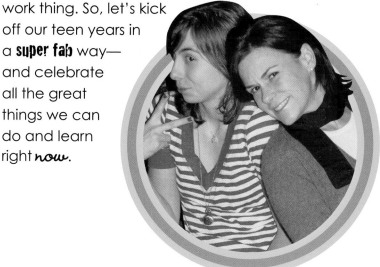

1. Build a fort for you and your buds (**no** sibs or parents allowed).

2. Drink a glass of Coke, while jumping on **one foot**.

STARS' WACKY 'N WILD HIDDEN TALENTS

Can you wiggle your ears? Or whistle through your nose? Just like us, some of our fave stars have got a knack for something weird. Hey, they didn't end up too bad!

DID YOU KNOW?

- Cameron Diaz can burp on command.
- Jessica Alba has a double-jointed backwards thumb.
- Kevin Jonas is double-jointed in every finger.
- Beyonce can flare her nostrils in two different places and wiggle her ears.
- Patrick Dempsey can juggle spinning plates.
- Jamie Foxx can rotate his eyeballs in a different direction.

9

Learn a few beauty tricks. Shake up your makeup and get a "*sa-weet*" party look.

CELEBRITY BEAUTY CONFESSIONS

"I learned the more blush you apply, the fuller your face looks. So if you want a more sculpted look, you don't want to use too much blush."

—Jennifer Hudson

13 is the perfect age to start experimenting with makeup...but no way should you raid your mom's! There's nothing cute, pretty, or age-appropriate about too much or the wrong shade. Try to keep it nice n' natural—red lips and dark eyeliner are big don'ts. A roll of gloss and hint of blush are just right for school. Come party time, score a flirty look. Sephora's beauty pro Jose Rivera got the deets on a young teen's beauty beat.

1. Blotting papers: Goodbye shine. These sheets take away excess oil without removing makeup. Stash a few in your locker or purse; they're perfect for everyday use. PICK: Clean & Clear Oil Absorbing Sheets.

2. Tinted moisturizer (with SPF): Teens don't need major coverage. A tinted moisturizer evens out complexion. Apply with fingers, blending from the center of the face outward. PICK: Laura Mercier Tinted Moisturizer.

3. Concealer: Got a zit? No worries! Give it a one-two punch with a medicated concealer. With your fingertip, dab a bit on the blemish to hide and heal at the same time. PICK: Murad Acne Treatment Concealer.

4. Cream blush: You can blend this easily with your fingers, and it looks younger than powder cuz' it's got a dewy finish. Look in mirror, smile, and put a dab on fingertips. Then apply to round part of cheeks in a circular motion toward your ears (but not all the way there). Stop when you see just a hint of color. PICK: Stila Convertible Color (doubles as a lip stain).

5. A neutral shadow: Gold or champagne are both good shades to make peepers pop. Or, try a sheer pastel. A shade similar to your eye color looks most natural. Use fingertips to apply, gently press into shadow and lightly dab across lid. PICK: LORAC's Serenity (shimmery bronze) or Urban Decay Urban Ammo Eye Palette (pastels)

Get Leighton's Look:

This Gossip Girl always has a fresh-faced look, even when she's hitting the party scene. Her makeup artist CHRIS COLBECK shares the 6 secrets to her superstar beauty—SO YOU CAN GET LEIGHTON'S LOOK!

1. Moisturize! It keeps skin hydrated and helps makeup go on easier. Then, cover up any blemishes with concealer. PICK: Chanel Ultra Correction Moisturizer & Laura Mercier Secret Concealer #2

2. Take a large brush and lightly dust bronzing powder all over your face. This gives skin a healthy glow. PICK: Lancôme Star bronzer

3. Use a glossy black mascara on top lashes only. Brush slowly upwards from the root to tip of lashes. Then, use a dark brown mascara on lower lashes; this color is softer and keeps the effect natural. PICK: Diorshow mascara in black on top lashes. Mac mascara in brown on bottom.

4. Sweep a silvery lavender eyeshadow on entire top lid. Also, apply just a touch of shadow to the inner corner of eyes to make your eyes pop. PICK: Lancôme Color Design eye shadow in Off the Rack.

5. Use a pinkish-apricot blush on the rounded part of cheeks to give 'em a natural, rosy glow. PICK: Chanel Blush in Rose Bronze.

6. Roll on a watermelon-colored gloss to give lips a flirty-girlie pout. PICK: Nars lip gloss in Frisky Summer. HINT: Apply lip balm before gloss for a longer-lasting shine.

"I really like eye shadows. It's always fun to put on a cute eye shadow that matches your outfit."

—Miranda Cosgrove

6. Clear mascara: Great stuff—it separates lashes and gives definition. Doubles as a brow gel. Pick: Make Up Forever Transparent Mascara

7. Lip gloss: A neutral pink or pale peach gloss compliments any look and works on all skin tones. Make thin lips look fuller by dabbing silver gloss onto the center of your lower lip. Pick: Sephora Super Shimmer Lip Gloss— comes in 16 girly shades.

SET OFF ON A GLOBAL ARMCHAIR ADVENTURE.

Today Show's **MATT LAUER** zips across the globe on his "Where In The World" adventures. While many of us won't be getting on a plane anytime soon, Matt took time out of his crazy schedule to share his 13 favorite places. Be inspired: We can all dream to hike it to at least one of these spots someday.

> "Traveling is a wonderful way to learn. If you can visit a place you learned about in school, you will appreciate it so much more. I am very fortunate I got to travel at a young age. It certainly enhanced who I am."
>
> —Hilary Duff

MATT'S 13 FAVE PLACES:

1. Greenland. **Head up to the Ilulissat Glacier. See firsthand what's at stake for our planet by coming face to face with the epicenter of the study of global climate change.**

2. Machu Picchu, Peru. **Take the time to soak in the genius of people who dared to dream, despite not having so many of the tools we all take for granted.**

3. African Safari. **Make a commitment to doing whatever you can to protect these magnificent animals, so your own children will one day be able to have the same experience.**

4. Paris. **Just have fun!**

5. Hawaii. **Visit the Kilauea volcano and allow yourself to feel absolutely powerless in the face of the real force of Mother Nature.**

6. Egypt. **See the great pyramids. I promise that no skyscraper will ever seem quite so impressive again!**

7. Australia. **Grab a swimsuit, a picnic lunch, and a camera and head to Bondi Beach. Just do it!**

8. Easter Island. **Check out all the Moai (which are statues carved out of volcanic ash). Then go to the highest point on the island. Turn and look around in 360 degrees and see what it's like to be truly isolated from the rest of the world.**

easter island

9. China. **Because I can think of 1.2 billion reasons why you are going to need to understand that country!**

10. New York City. **Head into Central Park with a Frisbee and go to the middle of the Sheep Meadow. Stop to consider the brilliance of the person who decided to put a park there in the first place!**

11. India. **Take a trip to Agra to see the Taj Mahal. Experience what falling in love can inspire someone to do.**

12. The Grand Canyon. **Stand at the edge and try to imagine what the first person who ever stood there must have been thinking!**

13. Washington D.C. **Take a tour of all the monuments that have been erected in honor of our founding fathers and former presidents. Consider their greatness, and then look for the place where you want us to build a monument to you and what you will achieve!**

13

JUST PLAY IT!

A juicy game of Truth or Dare is an awesome way to bond with your buds. It's up to you whether you 'fess or be the one who dares. If your friend asks for truth, try these—if dare, jump below.

Truth: Have you ever copied a celeb's outfit (head-to-toe) from a mag and worn it to school?

Truth: Have you ever lied to your BFF? Spill it! If so, what's the huge secret you're hiding?

Truth: Have you ever had a major crush on a friend's older brother? If so, who?

Truth: Have you ever laughed so hard you peed in your pants? What happened?

Dare: Prank call your crush and try to sell him something.

Dare: Dress up in a crazy outfit. Put on lots of makeup, tease your hair high, and go outside and say "hi" to 5 people.

Dare: Sing "Barbie Girl" out the window at the top of your lungs. Make it funnier by adding a little dance to it.

Dare: Mix ketchup, salt, pepper, mustard, and vinegar into a drink and take two big gulps.

"I always choose Dare! And one time I was dared to do a headstand at a club, and I had a dress on. I did it anyway."

—Avril Lavigne

6. Read! Read! Read at least one book a month (not on your homework list).

5 STEPS TO WRITING YOUR FIRST BESTSELLING NOVEL BEFORE YOU'RE 13

BY MICHAEL BUCKLEY, AUTHOR OF THE NEW YORK TIMES BESTSELLING SERIES, THE SISTERS GRIMM

1. This is easy. **First, read a lot of books! Stuff your noggin with anything you can get your hands on—fiction, memoirs, history, science, philosophy, current events, graphic novels, whatever. All of it will swirl around in your head and spin into ideas for stories.**

2. Once you have an idea for a story, write an outline briefly describing the beginning, middle, and end as well as all the important moments along the way. **(Sure, it's no fun but neither is going to the dentist—and you can't avoid either one.) It's very easy to get lost while writing a book and your outline will help keep you on track.**

3. Make sure your story is about something. **You might be writing about robots, killer chickens, super-powered lunch ladies, or unicorn-riding ninja princesses who fight zit monsters but what is the story really about? It's easy to write exciting stories but make sure your novel is also filled with themes, ideas, and values. Share with the reader how you see your world—even if you're writing about a world in a galaxy far, far away. By the way, don't steal any of those ideas, especially the ninja princesses. They're all mine!**

4. Once you have a first draft—rewrite your book! **The first draft of every book you have ever read was a horrible, unreadable disaster (except mine). Check your spelling and grammar and don't be afraid to move things around or cut out big parts that aren't working. Remember, the secret to good writing is rewriting.**

5. Once you're a published author sit back and wait for Hollywood to turn your really good book into a very bad movie. **See ...I told you it was easy!**

more

1. **Harry Potter** (series) by J.K. Rowling
2. **Twilight** (series) by Stephenie Meyer
3. *The BFG* by Roald Dahl
4. *Are You There God? It's Me, Margaret* by Judy Blume
5. **Little House On The Prairie** (series) by Laura Ingalls Wilder
6. **Dear Dumb Diary** (series) by Jamie Kelly
7. **The Baby-sitters Club** (series) by Ann Martin
8. **The Sisters Grimm** (series) by Michael Buckley
9. **The Magic Tree House** (series) by Mary Pope Osborne
10. *The Spiderwick Chronicles* by Holly Black & Tony DiTerlizzi
11. **Gossip Girl** (series) by Cecily von Ziegesar
12. *A Wrinkle In Time* by Madeleine L'Engle
13. *The View From Saturday* by E.L. Konigsburg

7. Buy your first bra. (I know, embarrassing, right?)

4-1-1

Go shopping with your mom for your first bra. Think of it as a bonding experience. Plus, it's a good time to bring up other "grown-up" stuff, like boys, dating, your period, and sex. I know it's all s-o-o-o-o hard to talk about, but moms were once TEENS too and they may actually have something smart to say!

BUZZWORTHY
8 out of 10 women wear the wrong size bra. Be sure to get fitted. Most department stores offer professionals who fit for free.

8. Choreograph **a dance** and put it on for your parents.

So, you can't shake it like Rihanna or rock it like The JoBros? No worries! We've all got our own rhythm— we just gotta let loose and find it. A good practice drill is to put on a show for your parents. Yup, there's no better audience (and confidence-booster) than smiling, clapping adults. Hip-hop choreographers TABITHA and NAPOLEON D'UMO reveal some parent-pleasing tips.

Select a tune your parents grew up on (i.e. Madonna, Michael Jackson, or MC Hammer).

Pick a dance they did when they were your age. Think cheesy 80s pop (i.e. Roger Rabbit, the Running Man, the Worm, or the Moonwalk).

Study steps. Update with the moves of today's stars.

Practice makes perfect. The more you go over the routine, the more likely you will avoid bumping into your fellow dancers.

If you're the choreographer, be patient if someone has trouble catching on. Teaching others a dance is a good opportunity to work on leadership skills. Think what works best for the group, not what moves make you the star.

Time to rock! Smile and make eye contact with your audience.

sLeep out in the woods, the mountains, the plains, or even your own backyard.

CAMPING 101!

Whether it's in the woods, at a camping site, or sleep-away camp —spending time in the great outdoors does a mind, a body, and a soul good. Pitching a tent, cooking over an open fire, or simply exploring nature are all eye-opening experiences that'll help us grow and appreciate mother earth. Ann Sheets works with the American Camp Association and she's got lots of handy camping hints:

more

1. Plan ahead: **Know where you're going and what is required. Get permission from the property owner or make reservations if you're going to a state park.**

2. Have the right equipment: **clothes, shoes, sleeping bag or bedroll, tent, and cooking gear.**

3. If you're cooking, be sure you can keep food safe before and after it's cooked (this may mean taking a cooler with ice, or using canned or freeze-dried food). Find out if there's a place to dispose of garbage, or if you'll need to take it with you when you leave.

4. Be prepared for emergencies: **Have a fully stocked first aid kit and know how to get help if you need it (take a cell phone along, with emergency numbers; make sure you can get cell reception).**

5. Before you go to a state park or campground, practice in your own backyard.
(If you forget a can opener and you're in the backyard, you can always go inside and get it. If you're at a campground and you forget something important, you may be out of luck.)

6. Take along an adult.

Want to go on a camping trip with your family or spend your summer at sleep-away camp? Check out **www.campparents. org**, the official Web site of the American Camp Association. You'll find lists of camps throughout the United States, plus hints on how to choose the right camp for you.

BEST EVER CAMP FIRE STEW

Serves: 10

Equipment needed: Dutch oven or kettle, large spoon, and a can opener

Ingredients:

- 2 lbs hamburger
- 1 small onion, diced (chop at home and pack in a Baggie).
- 2 cans tomato soup
- 2 cans mixed vegetables
- 2 cans diced potatoes
- Salt, pepper, seasonings to taste

Brown hamburger with onions. Drain grease. Add soup, mixed veggies, and potatoes. Simmer and season to taste. Enjoy!

10. Put on **Goth** makeup and scare your parents.

4-1-1 ON GOTH:

To some goth is a lifestyle (and we respect that), but to others it's a style—a very dark one.

Go goth for a day and watch your friends and family do a major double take.

Things you need:
Head-to-toe black clothes. A cape adds extra zing. Try a goth band tee, like The Cure or Marilyn Manson. Put on some high black boots and finish your look off with a studded choker.

Goth makeup is dramatic. Think red lips and dark eyeliner. And, of course, black fingernail polish.

11.   Baby-sit.

Fanstastic! You're old enough to baby-sit. Just remember, it involves a lot more than extra cash, a chance to 'raid somebody else's fridge, or paid-time to zone out in front of the TV. It's important to prepare; watching kids is serious biz. GENEVIEVE THIERS, Founder and CEO of www.Sittercity.com, shares these tips.

1. Before taking on a babysitting job, volunteer to be a Mother's Helper. This is great for work-from-home moms. They're still at home with the kids, but unable to pay full attention to them while working, so they need help.

2. Get a resume together and include all child care–related experiences, such as junior camp counselor, assistant soccer coach, and daycare volunteer.

3. Try to baby-sit only for families you know or who are recommended by friends.

4. It's never too early to get CPR-certified and trained in first aid so you can handle any emergencies with confidence.

5. Have a list of the child's allergies and emergency contact information just in case.

6. Ask the mom for a list of the kids' favorite toys and activities so you'll be able to calm them down quickly when they are upset.

7. Snack time can be fun time! Dress up bananas as banana-people. Use nuts and raisins to create a nutritious and entertaining snack.

8. Plan an adventurous scavenger hunt to find lost pirate treasure.

9. Gather all the kids' Play-Doh and toy kitchen items to play restaurant. Order foods like cookies, pancakes, and spaghetti and have the kids create them using all their Play-Doh ingredients.

10. Act out stories instead of just reading them.

11. Make cleaning up messy rooms fun by having a race to see who can clean up the fastest. Have an inexpensive reward ready, like stickers or DIY coupons ("next activity your choice" or "you earned a five-minute back massage").

12. When parents return, share a story about what you and the kids did—they will appreciate it!

13. Keep every drawing, painting, craft, and glue-covered mess that the kids make for you. You'll always smile when you look at them.

12.

Go on a shopping spree. Rev up your *style* with trendy accessories.

Rockin' style doesn't have to break the bank. Hats, scarves, or even a bold ring can make any outfit undeniably yours. Plus, lots of hip-super-cute accessories can be found in the $5, $10, or $15 zone. Fashionista **ALISON DEYETTE** has the scoop on how to perk up the same old outfit.

Belts: Wide, thin, studded—it's all in! Choose color, stripes, or patent leather—it's up to you. A wide belt looks great layered over a dress or long top. TRENDY! Or create a cinched waist by adding a skinny hot pink belt around your favorite long cardigan for a pop of color. FLIRTY!

Opaque Tights in solids like purple, red, green, and black. Also buy a few patterned pairs, like lace, argyle, and plaid. Looks super-cute paired with your fave mini—plus it's a style-smart way to wear your short skirt and not get the teacher's nasty glare.

Long scarves are a must. They come in lots of different colors, patterns, and textures, so you can mix and match. Be creative: use a long silky scarf as a belt or tie it around your head as a headband.

Jewelry: Multi-strand beaded necklaces, bangles piled on your wrist, dangly earrings, real or faux diamond studs, a leather cuff with a snap closure, a charm necklace, or your dad's old watch—the choice is yours. Hit up your local flea market, thrift store, or vintage shop to find unique pieces.

Sunglasses: Need we say more? A hip oversized pair gives you movie star cred!

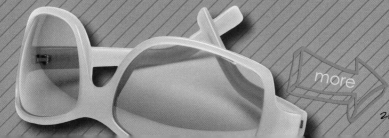

more

The Clique Girlz share their must-haves for all 13-year olds.

- A super shiny lip gloss.
- A diary to express their feelings throughout their life and experiences.
- A cell phone to stay in touch with friends.
- A cute purse.
- A great pair of heels.
- A really, really, really good pair of sunglasses.
- A good attitude of gratitude.
- A camera to remember special moments with friends and family.
- A carton of ice cream in your freezer.
- An all-time favorite book.
- A signature dance move.
- A true friend to share all of this with.

BUZZWORTHY

American teens spend almost $200 billion a year!

Cheap 'n Chic Shopping Destinations:

Claire's

Forever 21

H & M

Walmart

Target

JCPenney

dELIA's

Laila Rowe

For more tips: www.AliOnTheGo.com

13. Make a scrapbook. Include pics and other fun tidbits of/about your friends and family.

hotlist brittany's 13 fave scrapbook saves:

1. **Report Cards**
2. **Ticket Stubs**
3. **Celebrity Autographs**
4. **Postcards**
5. **Invitations**
6. **Birthday Cards**
7. **Pics of friends & family**
8. **Award Ribbons**
9. **Artwork**
10. **Brochures from places visited**
11. **Important journal entries**
12. **Tests you aced**
13. **Cool stuff to decorate your scrapbook (stickers, borders, drawings etc.)**

ADMIT ONE
810956
810956

POST CARD
M

FIRST PLACE

14. Discover your **talent** and work on it! Be it art, singing, acting, sports ...whatever!

WISE WORDS

Be motivated by your favorite star and don't be afraid to try new things. Soon you will discover that special something and will rule!

At 10, country cutie **TAYLOR SWIFT decided she wanted to be singer. From that point forward, she dedicated herself 100% to making her dream a reality. At 19, she's an award-winning superstar! And she shares with YOU her secrets to success.**

GAME PLAN:
"I started singing at festival and fairs and karaoke contests—anywhere I could. I begged my mom to take me to Nashville; eventually she did. I would walk into record labels alone, (my mom would wait in the car) and hand them my demo CD. I'd say "Hi I'm Taylor. I'm 11 and I'm looking for a record deal." ...I didn't get much response; so I returned to Pennsylvania and learned to play guitar and write songs.

SETTING GOALS:
"In order to develop and reach goals, I think it's important that you NEVER feel entitled to them. Take it one step at a time, because it's very rare people just get "discovered." It takes meeting lots of people and spreading the word and making connections and following paths that are sometimes dead ends. No matter what happens in life, no matter how many records you sell, be good to people. ...Being good people is a wonderful legacy to leave behind.

ADVICE TO OTHER DREAM-SEEKERS:
"If you've got a dream, it's your responsibility to make it happen. Do your research and find a way to be different than everyone else. Devote your time, devote your energy, and devote your talent. The rest is luck."

–Taylor Swift

"By the time you'e 13 you should develop and pursue a passion. I realize it takes a really strong work ethic and determination to pursue what I love—music. But, you also need focus and inspiration. And always remember to enjoy what you're doing."

–Nat Wolff

There's nothing unlucky about the number "13." Big things happened when these stars turned lucky 13.

Daniel Radcliffe scored a 3 million dollar payday for *Harry Potter & The Chamber of Secrets*

Golf sensation **Michelle Wie** became the youngest player ever to win the 2003 US Women's Amateur Championship.

Mary-Kate & Ashley Olsen executive produced their 1999 hit, *Passport to Paris*.

Miley Cyrus landed her breakout role on *Hannah Montana*.

GIRL POWER:

At 13, **BAILEY ROSE MONTE** scored her dream job. She's the *Today Show*'s teen reporter...an awesome gig! She interviews major stars, like Miley Cyrus, and covers "sweet" stories, like The Candy Expo. Bailey says it's hard work – but totally worth the effort. Think of her college apps—Rock On, Bailey! Here's her advice to go-get 'em teens, just like us.

"If you want something, it's up to you to make it happen. Don't rely on anybody else for motivation or inspiration. ... Never be afraid to take action: call or email for what you want. Yes, my aunt works at the *Today Show* (an advantage—I know), but if I didn't have this connection, I would have taken other steps to break into the business. ... That's why it's important to never burn bridges; the more people you know, the more help you will have in life. And if you're given an opportunity, you need to snatch it up and go for it!"

BAILEY AND MILEY: BAILEY IS IN THE PURPLE DRESS.

25

Eat broccoli—at least 10 pieces in one sitting.

When it comes to food keep it healthy and delicious ...dieting is so not necessary. Nutritionist **DANIELLE GETTY, R.D., CDN** says following these tips can help you feel and look your best!

• Bone up on Calcium: **Keep up your calcium intake—enjoy 3–4 servings of calcium rich food each day: good sources include skim or 1 percent low-fat milk, soymilk, low-fat cheese and nonfat/low-fat yogurts, calcium-fortified grains (cereal, frozen waffles and bars), tofu, beans, and broccoli.**

• Produce Rules: **Aim for 5 servings of fruits and veggies each day and try something new and unfamiliar like baby spinach in a salad, bok choy, or jicama.**

• Chug – that - Water: **Stick with water to stay hydrated. Aim for 6–8 glasses a day. It will help to keep your skin clear, muscles move, and all your organs functioning properly.**

• Keep it Lean: **Incorporate lean proteins into all of your meals. Fueling your body with protein helps to build and maintain muscle, boost your immune system, and keep you feeling and looking energetic and beautiful. Best bets: skinless chicken, turkey, fish and seafood, turkey burger, veggie burgers, egg whites, soy sausages, low-fat dairy, beans, tofu, chicken and turkey sausages, lean ham, and lean cuts of red meat.**

• Ditch the Junk Food: **Soda, candy, and fried food can make you feel yucky and zap your energy. Certainly enjoy these foods once in a while but it is best to save them for special occasions and outings with your friends.**

Dietary Guidelines
www.health.gov/dietaryguidelines/

My Food Pyramid
www.mypyramid.gov/guidelines/index.html

Health Information for Teens Around the World www.youngwomenshealth.org

16. Wear all the same color for the **entire day**— underwear included!

17. Play a prank on a friend.

Everyone's gotta know a good prank (or two). A harmless practical joke scores lots of laughs and no tears. *Access Hollywood's* BILLY BUSH describes himself as a devilish kid, and he's got the lowdown on Prank 101.

KEEP YOUR POKER FACE:
Never smirk, giggle, or be jumpy. Keep a cool, "nothing's up" attitude.

DON'T HURT ANYONE:
Pranks need to be harmless. Never endanger anyone with bodily harm (hurting others is not funny).

BE CREATIVE:
Make sure the prank is clever and nobody sees it coming!

NEVER EMBARRASS OTHERS:
We want to be laughing with them, not at them.

BE PREPARED FOR PAYBACK:
In the world of pranks, it's all about "I got you."

SAVE YOUR PRANKS FOR THE PEOPLE YOU LOVE:
Pranks are a sign of affection.

CLASSIC FIVE:

1. Put plastic wrap over the toilet seat.

2. Tape money to a string, let the victim see it, and pull it when he/she goes for it.

3. Put salt on your victim's toothbrush.

4. Place a styrofoam (not glass) cup filled with water above door frame. Let a third of the cup dangle off edge. Leave door ajar about 2" and wait for victim to enter.

5. When your victim is asleep, put his hand in warm water. Make 'em wet the bed.

more

STAR PRANKSTERS

Funny lady TINA FEY knows you're never too old for pranks. During the filming of *Baby Mama* the 38-year-old pulled pranks on her co-star and good friend Amy Poehler.

DANIEL RADCLIFFE (aka Harry Potter) is a major prankster. Once, the actor took his Harry Potter co-star, Robbie Coltrane's (aka Hagrid) cell phone and changed it so all the messages were in Turkish.

"I did a really funny prank where I got my assistant to paint all the cars in Amy's neighborhood a "washable" white so she would wake up... and think it was snowing. That was a good one."

—Tina Fey

18. Go to a **concert**.

TIFFANY GIARDINA is rocking the tween scene with her debut CD, "No Average Angel." The 14-year old pop star put together for YOU her list of 10 concert must-haves.

1. A t-shirt with the band's logo on it! There's no better way to tell your fave musician you love them.

2. Something sparkly. Wear a shirt with glitter, or a piece of jewelry, something that gets you noticed.

3. Wear your fave pair of jeans. Every girl feels their best in a comfy pair of jeans.

4. A backstage pass or an artist meet & greet. If you don't have a good contact to snag a backstage pass (few of us do), then enter a contest. Most artists sign up with a local radio station to do a fan meet & greet.

5. The artist's CD. I always bring a CD for the car, so on the way to the show I can get pumped up to see them perform.

6. Shoes that are comfortable and you can rock in! I love my boots, even though they have a heel, I can still dance and jump around.

7. A Sharpie. You never know when you can get your favorite artist's autograph – so best to be prepared.

8. Your knowledge of music! Sing along with your fave singer. I love when kids remember my lyrics and sing along.

9. Bring your BFFs. There are no better peeps to share your first concert experience. Take lots of photos.

10. A smile! I always throw a t-shirt to the fan with the biggest smile.

more

hotlist 13 songs to listen to before you're 13

1. "I Want to Hold Your Hand" by the Beatles (A classic song by a classic band)

2. "Material Girl" by Madonna (Because this is what your parents listened to at your age!)

3. "Hound Dog" by Elvis Presley (Because this is what your grandparents listened to at your age!)

4. "Imagine" by John Lennon (A timeless vision for a better world)

5. "Beautiful" by Christina Aguilera (Pay attention to the message and embrace your individuality)

6. "Hero" by Mariah Carey (Listen to the lyrics and find your inner strength)

7. "Blue" by LeAnn Rimes (The song that launched LeAnn's career at 13!)

8. "Thriller" by Michael Jackson (The title track from a landmark album)

9. "Pride (In The Name of Love)" by U2 (A timeless anthem)

10. "...Baby One More Time" by Britney Spears (Pure, innocent fun!)

11. "You Can't Always Get What You Want" by the Rolling Stones (Words to live by at any age)

12. "Just a Girl" by No Doubt (You can never get enough girl power)

13. "Respect" by Aretha Franklin (Nobody sings like Aretha!)

GET INVOLVED!

Most tweens have the heart and the will to volunteer, but we simply don't know how!!! Dosomething.org shares simple ways to make a difference.

1. Find a space in your neighborhood in need of some beautification, get a group together (with permission from your community board), and design a mural.

2. Connect with a local senior center and request a list of residents' birthdays. Work with friends and family to send birthday cards to each of your new friends.

3. Play with younger kids in an afterschool athletics program.

4. Donate your ponytail to help make wigs for children with cancer or other serious medical conditions.

5. Forego one birthday/Bat Mitzvah/Christmas gift this year and ask for a donation to be made in your name to your favorite charity.

more →

CELEBRITY DO-GOODERS

"I've worked with a lot of children's charities. ...When I come across a child out there that unfortunately is not doing well or is sick, whatever the circumstances are, it's to fun to be around them to kind of lighten the mood and cheer them up a bit. It's so fulfilling to me."

—Jesse Mccartney

"The most amazing adventure to seek out is volunteer work for a good charity/cause. It's an unbelievable feeling, to touch someone's life and make the world a better place at a young age."

—Maria Menounos

BUZZWORTHY Did you know 80 percent of tweens/teens want to volunteer, but only 20 percent do.

6. Talk with your school advisors and classmates to see if everyone will give $2 each month to help a needy child through Children International (www.children.org).

7. Donate a dress you no longer wear to someone who can't afford one for her own special party/birthday/event. Go to www.DonateMyDress.org.

8. Have a PSA (public service announcement) contest in your school. Break up into groups, pick your cause, design, direct, and broadcast your message.

GIRL POWER:

The Prudential Spirit of Community awards singled out these young teens for their super-hero strides and do-good missions. Volunteering will rev up your self-confidence and it sure looks strong on the college apps.

Riley, 14, of Bowling Green, KY, raises money for childhood cancer research with an annual day of lemonade sales. After her little brother lost his battle with cancer, Riley wanted to help others. She's raised $50,000 in 3 years, and does everything from making flyers, to getting supplies, to managing over 200 volunteers and 29 different stands.

Alexa, 14, of Mountville, PA, creates "Birthday in a Box" parties for kids living at a local homeless shelter. Alexa keeps track of birthdays, gets donations of cash, gifts, and party supplies from her community, and puts together "birthday boxes," so every kid there can have a party.

Alison, 13, of Fort Wayne, IN, is helping soldiers in Iraq. The seventh-grader collects large quantities of personal-care items, cookies, and letters of support and sends them to military facilities in Iraq.

Bria, 13, of Miami Gardens, FL, is a five-year cancer survivor, and wants to inspire other young cancer patients. After her cancer went into remission, she started a teddy-bear drive. The eighth-grader delivers the bears and shares her story with each patient to give them hope.

Be Active! Check out these websites.

www.dosomething.org
www.servenet.org
www.volunteermatch.org

20. Swim a whole lap underwater in a pool.

Heading into our teen years can be tricky stuff. For starters, what's happening to our bodies? Suddenly, we've got curves, our boobs are popping, and don't even get me started on mood swings. Yikes!!! Body Image Expert DR. ROBYN SILVERMAN assures us all is OK. Here's her top 10 list of changes that may be happening or will happen soon.

1. Breast buds: You'll notice your breasts are beginning to grow and get bigger. It may be time for a bra!

2. Hair …down there and everywhere: Pubic hair, underarm hair, and hair on our arms and legs starts to grow and get darker.

3 . Weight gain and changing shape: During puberty, it's normal to see the numbers on the scale go up, your waist get narrower, and your hips get wider and rounder.

4. Growing tall …and fast! Many girls have a big growth spurt. You may feel like all arms and legs! That's because your arms and legs grow first, and then your trunk catches up.

5. Get your period: Usually right after you see your breasts grow and you get a little taller, your first period will be on its way.

6. Cramps: Not the most comfortable part of puberty—but it sometimes comes with the territory! You may also feel bloated, tired, and achy.

7. Mood Swings: It's just like it sounds—one minute you can be happy and confident, the next, sad, sensitive, or irritable. This is called Premenstrual Syndrome or PMS.

8. Acne: Some girls will notice that their skin is oilier and they may see some blemishes on their face, shoulders, back, or arms.

9. Discharge: It may sound strange, but it's normal to get a thin, milky-white vaginal discharge when you're going through puberty.

10. Romantic feelings: You may start to feel attracted to someone else, want to hug them, touch them, or kiss them.

LEARN TO LOVE THE SKIN YOU'RE IN!

Flip through any mag and there are wa-y-y-y too many picture-perfect peeps. It's hard not to feel more Ugly Betty than American Princess. I know it's tough, but stop the negative self-talk and appreciate the skin you're in—no matter your size, skin color, or weight. Country singer KELLIE PICKLER shares how she (and others) can make themselves feel better.

SURROUND YOURSELF WITH POSITIVE PEOPLE:

Filter out the negative chatter. Nix girls who bash their bodies, and put down yours or other's weight. Positive and uplifting people make a world of difference. Surround yourself with those who support and encourage you.

DON'T COMPARE YOURSELF TO OTHERS.

I grew up really poor. My family was on food stamps. I was that girl in school who couldn't afford nice clothes, bags, or even braces. It took a while, but I learned it's not the goods you got, but who you are on the inside that counts.

Realize celebrity photos are fake.

Any celebrity who claims their photos are not air-brushed or touched-up is a liar. Mags Photoshop out freckles, cellulite, they make your boobs look bigger or smaller, your thighs slimmer—you name it. For the cover shot of my debut CD, Small Town Girl, they took out the bump in my nose—I was so mad, cuz the pic didn't look like me.

LOOK IN THE MIRROR AND APPRECIATE ALL YOUR GIFTS.

I used to hate my big butt. And I was super insecure about my nose and crooked teeth. But, as I got older, I realized these little imperfections are what make me special. Everybody can complain about something—stop it! Appreciate your gifts (like your health, family, and friends). Plus, I learned most people actually envy my curvy backside—it gives a gal some shape.

SPREAD A HEALTHY GIRL POWER MESSAGE.

I want to send a positive message through my music. My song "Don't You Know You're Beautiful" is all about realizing beauty comes from the inside. Sure, mags are always going to celebrate outer beauty, but try not to get hung up on it. In the long run, it's your smile, your attitude, and your smarts that count!

more

"I used to have really crooked teeth and they made my entire face look bad. Then, I got braces and it got worse! I would look in the mirror and see these snaggly, metal-clad teeth staring back at me. But, now that I've had my braces on for a while and my teeth are starting to straighten, I appreciate the extra sparkle my braces give to my smile (not to mention the major sparkle I will have once the braces come off)."

—Anna, 14, New Jersey

"I learned to appreciate the gap between my front teeth. I know a lot of girls hate their freckles, but I love mine and I don't know why some girls don't. They're so cute!"

—Emily, 10, Texas

"My arms are so skinny! But I learned to not care anymore. When someone looks at me they probably think I look really weak, but I'm not!

—Tori, 13, Minnesota

"I always wanted a smooth stomach (like the celebs have)! I finally realized thinking about it wasn't going to do anything. So, I started to eat healthier. Even though I still don't have my dream stomach, I am a lot happier and learned to say "So what?" to anyone who questions my confidence."

—Rebecca, 11, Vermont

BUZZWORTHY

• At age 13, 53 percent of American girls are "unhappy with their bodies." This grows to 78 pecent by age 17.

• 75 percent of teenage girls felt "depressed, guilty, and shameful" after just 3 minutes of looking at a fashion magazine.

Allykatzz.com is a go-to blog site for young teen girls. ...A hot topic is learning to accept yourself and your awesome individuality!

"I may not be the prettiest, but I learned to accept myself and stop comparing myself to others. That's one of the most important things you can learn in life."

— An Allykatzz from North Carolina

"I used to be so self-conscious of my body. I wouldn't want to wear certain things, or even look at myself in the mirror. But, in 8th grade I lost most of my baby fat and now I love my body. I didn't even go on a radical diet or over-exercise. All I did was make smarter choices. I say learn to love your body no matter what shape or size it is and make healthy choices."

—An Allykatzz from Connecticut

"I was chubby as a little girl, and was tormented by my peers. One girl in 2nd grade, when I was wearing shorts, walked up to me and told me my legs were 'meaty and fat.' I've learned to tell myself I'm not fat, because I'm not. I'm perfectly healthy."

—An Allykatzz from Texas

"I learned to love the fact I'm just a kid! I shouldn't be worrying about my weight, or nose, or hair. Plus, I don't have to worry about paying bills, or other adult situations. For now, I love that I'm young and have so many options ahead of me."

—An Allykatzz from Canada

22. Put on a fashion show and **rock** the runway.

Supermodel Strut

Fashion's most fabulous models all command the catwalk with their "take charge" stance. World famous runway coach J. Alexander, who teaches model wanna-bes to sashay on "America's Next Top Model," shares the 101 on the supermodel strut.

1. Fine-tune your posture. Keep shoulders back and push pelvis slightly forward.

2. Put one foot in front of the other. Toes should face forward. Your footprints should form a single line, as if you're walking on a rope.

3. Keep arms at your sides with a natural swing from front to back. Chin should be lifted up a little and not pointed out. Look straight ahead.

4. A basic smile of confidence always works on the runway.

5. The key is not to trip in your heels. If you do fall, get up quickly, flash a big smile, and keep on strutting.

"Be confident and fearless with fashion. Fabulosity is celebrating who you are and your individual greatness"

—Kimora Lee

23. Have an OMG moment and learn from it!

"I was riding my bike and I saw my crush. I wanted to impress him, so I started riding with no hands. I looked back to see if he was noticing me, and I crashed straight into a tree. He and his friends started cracking up. And, I was mortified."

—Tamsen, 13, Massachusetts

Spill a drink on your crush. Flub your lines in the school play. Or score a goal for the other team. We've all had an O-M-G moment—and felt totally mortified! But these red-faced moments can actually be good for you—and make you a wiser and stronger person!

Cheetah Girl SABRINA BRYAN and her writing bud JULIA DEVIL-LERS, co-authors of *Princess of Gossip*, have had their share of humiliating experiences. Sabrina says actors have OMG moments all the time—you've seen some of them on the bloopers at the end of the show! Actors don't expect to get things the first try—that's why they have retakes, where they shoot scenes over and over again. Julia says some of her OMG moments have made great stories, and although JULIA they're weren't fun at the time, girls always tell her how much they can relate to those scenes.

Remember that failure happens to everyone—it's how you respond that matters. Sabrina and Juila share their bounce-back secrets:

• Think about what just happened. It's a good opportunity to consider what went wrong and how you could do it differently next time.

• And yes, there should be a next time. Give it a second chance. Or third. …Giving up because it doesn't come easily is just letting yourself down. It's so rewarding to work harder than you have before, and actually reach it. Think about how great it would be if you do try again and next time, succeed!

• And if you don't succeed, cheer yourself on just for trying!

• Don't lose perspective. It's easy to think you'll feel like this forever… but you won't. Move forward.

• Don't lose confidence! Just because it didn't work this time, does not mean you're a loser.

• Failure can make you appreciate your support system. Your parent, a trusted friend, your diary, or even a pet can help you feel better. Sharing your OMG moments can be a bonding experience and help you connect with others who have been through similar times.

• Failure can teach you the importance of hard work. Sure some things will come easy to you, but it's the ones that take effort—and yeah, sometimes failure along the way—that show you hard work pays off!

"I am a fairly experienced horseback rider. …One time a photographer was taking pictures of me riding as I was practicing an emergency dismount. At that exact moment, my shirt got caught on the saddle horn, it hiked up to my chin and my bra ripped in two and I fell on my butt. Although I was mortified, I was able to laugh it off, and I learned even though it was horrible at the time, it could be (and is) one of my funniest memories and best stories to share.

— Julia, 13, Ohio

DIY BUSINESS IDEAS:

Why not turn your passion into a money-making biz? From the simple weekend lemonade stand to petsitting to creating websites, you're never too young to start raking in the dough. Like volunteering, this too looks good on college apps. Take 30-something JENNIFER KUSHELL—she started her first biz at 13, painting and selling t-shirts. Now, she's on her 8th biz as the co-founder of www.ysn.com—a go-to resource for young business execs. Here are her suggestions on how to tap into the young entrepreneur in all of us.

1. Take a good look around. Find a need or problem that you can solve, that people would be willing to pay you for. Some ideas: sell candy or jewelry to your friends, shovel snow, or take on special projects for your neighbors.

2. Size up the competition. Look for other businesses similar to yours. Figure out what you can do better, how you can be more cost effective, and how to get the word out about your biz.

3. Research your opportunity & audience. Get to know your audience. Even if you're building a product or service that you know others need, it's still important to ask your prospective clients questions.

4. Build a plan. Once you know what kind of business you want to start, begin building your plan. Know 1) what the product or service is, 2) your pricing strategy or price list, 3) who your target customers are, 4) how you plan to market to them, 5) your start-up costs (all the things you need to start the business), 6) how you plan on making money (Sales Price - Cost per unit or service = Profit). Then think about how many items or services you can sell over one month, two months, three, and project what your sales would be.

5. Create your business brand and marketing materials. Every business needs a great name and logo. That's the brand you'll want everyone to know about! Use your name and logo graphic on everything that represents your business. Be sure to describe what you do, your product or service. Create business cards and fliers that you can pass out to prospective clients and post around your community. You can also create a web page or online profile. Be sure to always include contact information, like a phone number or email address. Never give your physical home address though. Check with your parents before promoting any personal information to stay safe.

BUZZWORTHY

• 71 percent of students, age 13–18 want to be self-employed at some point.

• 41 percent of kids age 9–12 want to start their own business.

25.

Do a facial—make it out of stuff in your kitchen

Raid your fridge for the best beauty goodies. Our buds at the eco-cool site PLANET GREEN share their favorite au natural treats.

THINGS YOU NEED:

- Wash cloth
- Clean dry towel
- Mixing bowl
- Spoon
- Whisk
- Ingredients for mask chosen

LEMON EGG WHITE MASK

Good acne-buster. The egg white soaks up excess oil and the lemon helps get rid of minor facial discoloration.

1. Crack an egg and remove yolk. Beat egg whites in bowl.

2. Cut a fresh lemon in half and squeeze into bowl, mixing it in with egg white to form a paste.

3. Apply to clean face, avoiding eye area, and let sit for 15–20 minutes. Rinse face and pat dry with towel.

HONEY & ALMOND SCRUB:

Good for all skin types to cleanse, exfoliate, and moisturize.

- 1 tbs honey
- 1 tsp plain yogurt
- 2 tbs finely ground almonds
- ½ tsp lemon juice

Mix everything together. Rub gently onto face, avoiding eye area, for 1–2 mins. Rinse off with warm water.

OATMEAL HONEY MASK:

Works well on all skin types and gives complexion a glow. The oatmeal and yogurt gets rid of dead skin cells, while the honey moisturizes and tightens pores.

INGREDIENTS:

- 2 tbs plain yogurt (the fattier the better)
- 1 tbs honey
- 1–2 tbs cooked & cooled oatmeal

Mix everything together until it forms a smooth paste. Spread over face, avoiding eye area, and leave on for 10–15 mins. Wash off with a warm washcloth.

TRY OTHER FOOD COMBOS:

Avocado+Honey
Banana+Yogurt+Honey
Oatmeal+Olive Oil
Egg Yolk+Honey+Olive Oil
Strawberries+Cream+Honey
Brown Sugar+Milk

26. Have a down 'n' dirty food fight.

hotlist brittany's favorite food flyers

1. **Spaghetti:** Easy to throw. Awesome splatter factor when it hits target.

2. **Milk, Water, or Juice:** Need to be close, and pour. Major points if victim drenched.

3. **Cupcakes:** Get a good a grip and throw. Cupcakes are awesome for long-distance destinations.

4. **Eggs:** Mess factor is huge. Be careful: these oval missiles can hurt.

5. **Tomatoes:** Good for the long-distance haul. Messy upon impact.

6. **Chocolate Pudding:** Throw it anywhere, makes a mess where ever you throw.

WISE WORDS: Unless you want to be grounded or in detention for life, take your food fights outside.

27. Keep a **journal** or a diary

And keep it under lock and key. Journaling lets you celebrate you. It's an awesome way to let out your feelings, get a reality check, discover who you are and keep track of how you've changed. Be sure to protect against snooping sibs and stash it out of sight. Your private thoughts need to be just that—PRIVATE!

more

...NOT SURE WHAT TO WRITE ABOUT? HERE ARE 13 IDEAS TO GET YOUR BRAIN PUMPING.

"I was so scared *when...*"

"I've never been happier than *when...*"

"My favorite place in the world *is...*"

"I've never been more embarrassed than *when...*"

"My best friend really upset me when she *did...*"

"Someday I will be wonderful *at...*"

"My parents really bug me when *they...*"

"What's the best thing about *being 13...*"

"What's the worst thing about *being 13...*"

"If I had a million dollars, I *would ...*"

"If you could be any celebrity, who would it be and *why...*"

"If you could be invisible, who would you spy on *why...*"

"My wish for the future *is...*"

Hint: Frequent journaling makes you a better writer. Spend 15-20 mins everyday writing down your thoughts/happenings. A good time is right before you go to bed.

Go old skool and pick up a pen and write a letter. Yes, it's old-fashioned, but everybody likes to receive snail mail—and it certainly shows you care! Co-host of *The View* and mother of two, **ELISABETH HASSELBECK** shares two peeps all teens need to write to.

Write the following letters:

(on paper, in an envelope, with a stamp—NO E-Mails!)

1. To your parents—about what you love about them, even though they often say "no."

2. To yourself—to open when you have kids one day—so that you never forget what it was like to hear "no."

28. Learn To Love Math.

IF FRACTIONS, MIXED NUMBERS, AND GEOMETRY GET YOUR HEART RACING (AND NOT IN A GOOD WAY) —*YOU'RE NOT ALONE!* MATH HAS A BAD RAP. ...SO, NOT WORTHY! NUMBERS AREN'T JUST FOR NERDY DUDES. GIRLSTART, A GROUP DEDICATED TO MAKING MATH COOL, SUMS UP FIVE REASONS WHY FAB GALS, LIKE YOU, LOVE MATH!

1. Math is Cool! Did you know that some of the coolest girls out there are really math goddesses? If you love math, you'd be hanging out with Danica McKellar (*The Wonder Years*), Teri Hatcher (*Desperate Housewives*), and Lisa Kudrow (*Friends*).

2. Math is Fun! Try out this equation and have a blast. Take 1 teaspoon of Borax ™ + 1 cup water + 2 tablespoons of white glue = BEST SLIME FEST EVER!

3. Math is Exciting! Math can be mind-blowing. For example, if you sent 10 text messages a day starting at age 13, and continued until you were 60 years old, you will have sent 171,550 total text messages!

4. Math is Real! How can you possibly grow your wealth and track of all that cold hard cash if you can't add, add, add? Math can bring out your inner mogul!

5. Math is Musical! Think about it. Math is the basis for music and dancing. It's where rhythm comes from! It's about beats, steps and timing. Having fun with math will boost your creative juices, and get you in the groove!

29. Know how to create a **knockout** (yet age-appropriate) hairstyle.

GOT A HOT PARTY AND NO CLUE HOW TO STYLE YOUR HAIR? DON'T STRESS, ADRIANA LIMA'S MANE DUDE, DOMINIC PUCCIARELLO, SHARES SOME EASY-TO-DO YET MODEL-WORTHY LOOKS FOR A GIRL'S NIGHT OUT!

more

Chic n' Curly:

Don't mess with Mother Nature. Work with your curly hair and create a playful side-swept updo.

Get the look:

1. Take a quarter-size amount of a styling cream and apply to hair with finger-tips, start at ends and work way up to scalp. Helps tame frizz.

2. Best to air-dry curls. If pressed for time, attach a diffuser to blow-dryer, and without touching hair, apply heat section by section.

3. After hair is dry, if some pieces seem less curly, use a curling iron (ideal barrel size is same as your curls or one size smaller). Gently wrap uncurled strand of hair around iron; don't clamp down on curls.

4. Loosely pull hair back into a side ponytail; be sure not to tie too tight.

Optional: Side-swept bun Divide pony into sections. Take individual strands and bobby pin section by section to the base of the pony; until all pieces are tucked into a bun. Lightly mist with hairspray to hold in place. Don't worry if looks messy – it's supposed to have that effortlessly cool edge.

more

43

Fabulous Waves:

Relaxed n' bouncy curls give wavy-haired girls a glam slam that's perfect for any special event.

Get the look:

1. Spritz a detangling spray on towel-dried hair from roots to end. Get a fistful of hair and scrunch allover.

2. Air-dry hair. Or, pull it back into a loose bun, and blow-dry bun. Then, take it out and use your fingers to fluff out waves.

3. Enhance natural wave with a large-barrel curling iron; curl front section in the direction away from face. In back and on the sides, alternate the direction of the curl, one facing towards the face, the next away. Wrap only the bottom ends, or wrap roots to ends for a curly look.

Optional: Half up/Half down Take the hair on top of head section from temple to temple and brush this section in the direction away from face. Pull it back and when almost to the crown do a little twist and secure with pretty bow or jeweled barrette.

Wrapped Pony: This is a simple yet girlie chic updo for straight-haired gals who want to add sass to their ponies' swing.

Get the look:

1. Pull your hair back into a tight pony at the center of your head.

2. Make sure there are no bumps when brushing back. You want it to look smooth 'n' sleek. Leave out a few strands if you prefer some fringe in front.

3. Take a strand of hair, not too thick, from underneath pony and wrap it around hair tie. Secure with bobby pins underneath and make sure the ends of strands are hidden.

4. Mist a glitter spray over the whole 'do to give it sparkly shine.

30. Make a **tasty** treat for your BFF's b-day.

Home-made cupcakes are a sweet gift. Jazz up the icing with a tasty topper from baking dudes MATT LEWIS and RENATO POLIAFITO, owners of NYC's Baked.

● Try a mini candy on top of your favorite icing. Mini peanut butter cups or Oreos are tasty treats.

● Nix the icing. Instead top it with a small scoop of your favorite ice cream—and then top that with sprinkles.

● Mash up a peppermint patty or Junior Mints and mix into buttercream icing for a cool blast.

● Try something salty. Crushed pretzels taste awesome on chocolate cupcakes.

● Skip the icing. Instead dab on marshmallow Fluff, a drizzle of chocolate, and some crushed graham crackers on chocolate cupcake for a yummy s'mores treat.

More Sweet Trix:
www.bakednyc.com

31. Get **Organized**.

HOMEWORK. CELL PHONES. IPODS. BOOKS. IF YOU'RE LIKE MOST TEENS, YOU'VE GOT A LOT OF STUFF! ...KEEPING TRACK OF IT ALL CAN BE EXHAUSTING—IF NOT IMPOSSIBLE! AT LEAST FOR ME, I AM ALWAYS LOSING AND FINDING AND LOSING SOMETHING! DAWN WINDSOR, FOUNDER OF WINDSOR VIRTUAL OFFICE SOLUTIONS HAS SOME GET IT TOGETHER TIPS.

1. Bedrooms—**WHAT FLOOR???** Spend just five minutes a day either putting things in their rightful places; your sweaters folded, your dirty laundry in the hamper, and neatly stack your books on the corner of your desk.

2. Chaotic Closets—**YIKES...DO NOT OPEN THAT DOOR...**One of the easiest and most cost-effective ways of organizing your closet is to be sure everything is hung up on hangers.

3. Droopy Drawers—**JUST STUFF IT!** Try designating each drawer to a specific group of clothing. For example: 1st drawer for only undergarments, socks, 2nd drawer for night time wear/lounging house clothes, 3rd drawer for tops that do not require hanging and the 4th for pants and bottoms that do not stay on hangers.

4. Morning Mayhem—**GET UP, GET DRESSED & GET OUT!** 3 simple ways to help you get out of the house on time: Lay out your clothes the night before, make your lunch before bed, and place your school bag (with the finished homework) by the front door.

5. Tiny Technologies—**WHERE'S MY????** Have a designated spot to put your iPod, cell phone, or MP3 player in every single day when you come home.

45

32. Don't Wash your hair for 3 days. Ewww!

> **BUZZWORTHY** Celebs often skip the shampoo on a big party night. It's easier to style an updo or create fab waves with hair that's not squeaky clean. Hair's natural oil helps hold style longer.

33. Make a friend outside your **neighborhood**.

What makes us gals super-fab is that we all come in different sizes, shapes, and colors. So, keep the sisterhood strong and never snub someone cuz they live in different hood or don't look like you. Teen superstar SELENA GOMEZ lives by the golden rule: **Treat others like you wanted to be treated.**

selena's
judgment-free world

1. It seems like today the world is consumed with blogging and being obsessed with judging what people do in their life. It's hard to not let words or judgment affect you—gossip isn't fair.

2. Gossip usually comes from people who don't even really know you, never even had a conversation with you.

3. To avoid the pain of gossip (and judgmental peeps), surround yourself with people you would be proud to be.

4. Don't judge, step back, and realize everyone is her own individual. What may be good for you may not be good for them. You are not there, you are not them.

34. Express *yourself* with a cool cyberspace profile. Be sure to keep it private—limit access to only your closest buds.

The web is an awesome place to do research, play a game, blog, or simply chat with friends. 95 percent of teens say they've belonged to a social network (i.e. Facebook, MySpace, Club Penguin). Yet, you gotta play it smart. Just like in our off-line life, not everyone is nice and some websites are not safe. KIDPOWER, an internet safety group, shares these 13 tips to cyber safety.

1. Never post anything on the internet or send something electronically that you don't want the world to see, including parents, teachers, and colleges.

2. Remember that the internet is no different than the street—people are still strangers in a public area.

3. Be aware that, even if you know someone, you cannot control what that person might do with any information given through the internet, including using it in ways that might be embarrassing to you.

4. Most people who bother kids on the internet pretend to be another kid with similar interests. Be aware that you cannot tell whether a person is telling the truth online. A man of 60 can easily pretend to be a girl of 13.

5. Do not accept friend requests on social networking sites from people you do not know. On most sites, by accepting someone as a friend, you give him or her direct access to any information in your profile and the opportunity to add things to your profile.

6. Always check with your parents first before putting any personal information on the internet by filling out a survey, registering on a Web site, joining a chat group, etc.

7. Personal information is more than just your name and where you live; it includes photos, where you go to school, your telephone number, the names of friends or family or teachers, sports team, neighbors, etc.

8. Have the courage to speak up if you notice any cyber cruelty. Say that this is wrong and that you are not going to keep it a secret.

more

9. Always get permission from your parents before you accept gifts from, have a telephone conversation with, or make a plan to meet someone you don't already know well, whether you learned about that person through the internet or any-where else.

10. If anyone starts to initiate sexual or threatening talk or if a Web site starts to show some-thing sexual or graphically violent, stop the contact and let your parents know.

11. To avoid giving out any personal information, use email addresses that do not have your name as part of the address.

12. Always check with your parents before opening or replying to any kind of spam and before opening any kind of attachments. It is best to delete spam emails immediately.

13. Anytime you have a problem on the Internet, tell an adult you trust and get help.

BUZZWORTHY

• 58 percent of teens don't think posting photos or other personal info on social network is unsafe. Amaziingly, 64 percent post photos or video of themselves, while more than half post their address. (Reality check, people!)

• 42 percent of parents don't monitor what their children read or type in chat rooms

Check out these web safety resources:
www.kidpower.org
www.webwisekids.org
www.onlinesafetysite.com
www.ypulse.com

hotlist brittany's fave socialnetworking sites:
• Facebook • Stardoll • Club Penguin

35. Try archery until you get a bullseye.

36.

Make a mini-movie with your friends—get goofy.

Making movies—just like journaling or writing a poem—is a terrific way to get out your feelings and document YOUR LIFE. Movie producer DEBRA MARTIN CHASE is Hollywood's "Queen of Tween." As the force behind hit movie series like *Princess Diaries*, *The Cheetah Girls*, and *Sisterhood of The Traveling Pants* (check out the cast shot!), Debra's message on- and off-camera is "you have the power to be yourself and the power to do anything you want." If that special something is to be the next great moviemaker, here are Debra's tips to consider before you shout-out Lights, Camera, Action.

KNOW YOUR LEAD CHARACTER:

Ask yourself a few simple questions: What motivates my character? What is her journey? What is the message of the film? Even if you're just documenting a day-in-the-life of your buds, know who and what the focus is.

BE PREPARED TO LEAD:

Create a team. Find someone to write (if not you), act, and someone to pull together costumes and props. Inspire your crew with enthusiasm and a solid production plan.

Have a go-with-the-flow attitude. Realize, despite your best efforts, things will go wrong. Keep your cool.

DON'T LISTEN TO CRITICS:

Art is subjective. Also, my greatest lessons came from failures. Review work later on and find things to improve. If you never try to make a film, you will never develop your potential. Everything is hard work, and the people who make it look the easiest probably worked the hardest.

BE PROUD:

Creating a film is a great thing to share with others. Plus, it's a good way to record the different stages of your life.

49

BE INSPIRED BY YOUR FAVORITE "GREEN" CELEB

"Grow some sprouts. And, learn about perma-culture, which will teach you how to grow your own garden or even build a natural house. It's important to do something good for our environment."

–Ellen Page

"As teens, it's up to us to encourage our friends to go green. I eat organically and I pick up trash when I see it."

–Cody Linley

13 Ways to be a "Little Miss Green"

IT'S UP TO US TO KEEP OUR PLANET HEALTHY FOR A FUTURE GENERATION OF TWEENS. CELEBRITIES ARE MAKING A "GO GREEN" DIFFERENCE AND SO CAN YOU! WWW.TREEHUGGER. COM REVEALS HOW TO BE A PART OF THE ECO-MOVEMENT.

1. Be inspired by Hayden Panettiere: Protect the animals! The Heroes cutie sells her own "lightly worn" clothes and accessories on her Web site, www.panettierecloset.com, to raise money to save the dolphins.

2. Conserve energy! Turn off your computer off at night. Unplug your cell phone charger, desk lamp etc. when not in use! Up to 40 percent of your home's monthly energy use is "phantom energy." That's a lot of wasted electricity!

3. Save the forest and nix the plastic! Pack your lunch (or snack for on-the-go) in a reusable sack, instead of a brown paper bag, and use small Tupperware containers instead of Zip-loc bags. Also, get your parents to use a canvas bag at the grocery store.

4. Be Less Trashy! Use refillable water bottles. Buzzworth factoid: 8 out 10 bottles used end up in a landfill.

5. Save water! Don't leave the faucet running when you brush your teeth. Keep shower time to a minimum.

6. Go organic! Let parents know which fruits and vegetables are the most important to buy organic, by checking out the Environmental Working Group's Dirty Dozen (www.ewg.org/sites/foodnews/walletguide.php)

7. Save the wildlife! Buy vintage clothes. You'll help cut-down on resources used to make new clothes. Plus, there are super cool finds at thrift stores.

8. Use cosmetics and beauty products not tested on animals. Educate yourself: log onto onto www.caringconsumer.com to find out who tests and who doesn't.

9. Be smart on global warming! Read *The Down-to-Earth Guide to Global Warming*. It's packed with kid-friendly suggestions.

10. Use rechargeable batteries with your iPods, cell phones, and PSPs. When batteries go kaput, don't throw them in the trash. Take them to a recycling center instead.

11. Cut down on waste! Share your stuff like games, books, clothes, and DVDs. This is a great way to reduce clutter and the garbage you create.

12. Draw your blinds or shut your curtains during long summer days... this will keep your bedroom cool. In the winter, let the sun shine all day long to heat your space naturally.

13. Reduce, Reuse, Recycle: The 3 Rs are the biggest rules in being green. Reduce waste wherever possible. Reuse what you can. Recycle what's left over.

More Green Tips:

www.treehugger.com

www.green4teens.com

www.green.yahoo.com

38.

Play a neighborhood-wide **game** of "Ghost in the Graveyard' or "Flashlight Tag" or "Hide'n Seek"

DON'T SPEND 24-7 ON THE COMPUTER (SO NOT COOL, NOT TO MENTION UNHEALTHY). GET YOU AND YOUR BUDS' BUTTS OUTDOORS. EXPERIENCE THE CLASSIC GAMES YOUR PARENTS GREW UP ON.

GAME RULES 101: GHOST IN THE GRAVEYARD

1. Gather up your friends. Best time to play is after dusk.

2. Find a spot to play. The best is a field or big backyard. Mark a home base.

3. Choose someone to be the ghost. Everyone else starts on home base, and the ghost hides.

4. The ghost counts out loud to twelve o'clock and then screams midnight and leaves home base.

5. If and when you see the ghost shout "'Ghost In The Graveyard" and run back to home base. If the ghost tags you before get there, you become the ghost

More Old Skool Games: (ask your parents how to play) Flashlight Tag, Kickball, 4 Square

39.

Appreciate time *alone.*

Sometimes you just gotta chill. Whether it's friends, family, or homework overload that's got your brain buzzing—take a T-O (timeout). Spend some quality time alone and MEDITATE. Sound way too Zen? Don't knock it 'til you try it! Experts say meditation reduces stress, increases energy, and fires up your brain. New York city yogini OCEANA shows us how to just breathe.

more

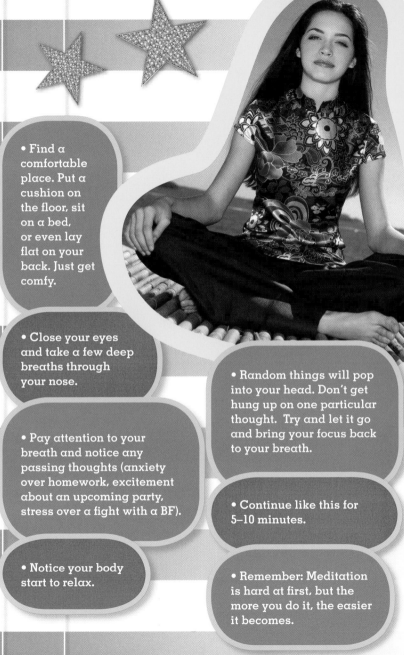

- Find a comfortable place. Put a cushion on the floor, sit on a bed, or even lay flat on your back. Just get comfy.

- Close your eyes and take a few deep breaths through your nose.

- Pay attention to your breath and notice any passing thoughts (anxiety over homework, excitement about an upcoming party, stress over a fight with a BF).

- Notice your body start to relax.

- Random things will pop into your head. Don't get hung up on one particular thought. Try and let it go and bring your focus back to your breath.

- Continue like this for 5–10 minutes.

- Remember: Meditation is hard at first, but the more you do it, the easier it becomes.

40. Watch the **entire** *Titanic* movie…yes, the whole 194 minutes.

hotlist brittany's **13** fave flicks

1. *Harry Potter*
2. *Star Wars*
3. *Clueless*
4. *Charlie and the Chocolate Factory*
5. *Freaky Friday*
6. *Mean Girls*
7. *Legally Blonde*
8. *Pirates of the Carribean*
9. *ET*
10. *The Princess Diaries*
11. *The Parent Trap*
12. *The Wizard of Oz*
13. *Big Fat Liar*

41. Trade already chewed gum with your best friend.

42. Make a massive sundae and **pig out!**

BEST SUNDAE TOPPINGS

Who doesn't like a yummy Cold Stone Creamery treat? Ray Karam, the lucky dude who gets to think up all those sweet sensations, dishes on how to create the ultimate combo:

"Start with Cake Batter ice cream flavor and mix in the most chocolaty rich ingredients in the store, including Heath Bars, Kit Kats, M&Ms, Reese's Peanut Butter Cups and Snickers. For a little extra zing, top it off with a few swirls of rich fudge and serve in a chocolate candy-coated waffle bowl."

My buds and I love to create massive sundaes. Who doesn't? Girl talk and ice cream—what a yummy combo.

"mint ice cream, with Oreos, bananas, chocolate chips, gummy bears, rainbow sprinklers and topped with chocolate sauce."

—claudia, 13

"vanilla ice cream with bananas, peanut butter, hot fudge, and chocolate.....like chocolate chips and chocolate bars.... but lots of CHCOLATE!!!"

— Morgan, 13

"mint chocolate chip and chocolate ice cream with Oreos, hot fudge, strawberries, and M&Ms.

—Lauren, 12

"double fudge ice cream, with chocolate sprinkles, cherries, M&Ms, Oreos, cookie dough, Snickers, Heath Bar, pecans, bananas, cake, peppermints and cinnamon, topped with caramel, whipped cream and chocolate sauce."

—Lauren, 13

"And MINE IS... mint chocolate chip ice cream, chocolate fudge ice cream, Snickers, dark chocolate bar, Oreos, chocolate chip cookies, marshmallows, hot fudge, caramel, whipped cream, cherries, and chocolate sprinkles!!!"

—Brittany

43. Chill with *yoga*.

STRIKE A POSE! GIVE YOUR MIND, BODY, AND SPIRIT A TUNEUP! YOGA TEACHER MICHELLE BARGE AND HER STUDENTS AT NEW YORK CITY LAB SCHOOL & MUSEUM SCHOOL SHARE WHY ALL YOUNG GIRLS SHOULD GET WITH THE PRACTICE. O-H-H-H-MMMMM!

1. Yoga is "ME" time that's parent-approved.

2. Some of your favorite celebs do yoga: Cameron Diaz, Melissa Joan Hart, Mary-Kate Olsen, Angelina Jolie, Sarah Jessica Parker, and the Dixie Chicks!

3. Yoga builds strength.

4. Yoga is a great way to meet people.

5. Yoga teaches discipline and self-respect.

6. Yoga helps you see the world from another viewpoint.

7. Yoga helps make a difference in the world by becoming SELF-aware.

8. You experience a "chilled-out" but "can-do" feeling after practice.

9. Yoga can help you do better in other sports.

10. Yoga teaches you to love and respect your body.

11. Yoga allows you to concentrate better, longer, and deeper.

12. Yoga is a non-competitive activity.

13. In yoga you always come in at first place.

BUZZWORTHY
Yoga may seem like the hot new trend, but it was first practiced in India over 5,000 years ago.

44. Get an awesome report card that will make your parents smile.

You've got a science test on Thursday—the same day as your big math exam and your book report is due. Are your teachers nuts? How can they expect you do all that, please! First, calm down and breathe! Go-to experts WWW.KIDSHEALTH.ORG share their no-fail tips for sure-fire success.

START STUDYING IN SCHOOL
Good study techniques begin in the classroom as you take notes. Some keys to note-taking are to write down facts that a teacher mentions or writes on the board during class.

TIME MANAGEMENT
When you sit down to study, think about how much time you want to devote to each topic. This will keep you from getting overwhelmed. For example, a weekly Spanish verb test probably won't be as intense as a big history test.

HOW TO STUDY
As you study, review your notes and any special information from your textbook. In the case of math or science problems or equations, do some practice problems. Many teachers tell students ahead of time what the format of an exam will be. This can help you tailor how you study. Read things over several times if you need to, and write down any phrases or thoughts that will help you remember main ideas or concepts.

GIRL POWER:

"Learn to love school. Too many of us, spend so much time complaining about it. Why not do your homework instead of complain, at least it will be done. 'kay fine you don't have to love school, but at least give it a try—it's not as bad as liver or anything."

—An Allykatzz

I'LL STUDY TOMORROW AND OTHER EXCUSES
It's tempting to put off studying until the last minute (also known as procrastination). If you're a procrastinator (and who isn't sometimes?), one of the best ways to overcome it is by staying organized. Keep your notes organized, stay on top of required readings, and follow the other study tips mentioned above to stay focused and in control.

THE PAYOFF
When you've finished studying, you should feel like you can approach the test or quiz with confidence—not necessarily that you will get 100 percent of the answers correct, but that you have a good understanding of the information.

More Study Tips: www.KidsHealth.org

45. Hang with your MOM (or a special older female in your life)!

Moms can be annoying, embarrassing, not always understanding—but they will always be there and love you—unconditionally. And like it or not, most of us will someday grow up to be a lot like our mothers. So, why not get to know her a little better. KATIE HAVARD writes an advice column with her mom, Melissa, called "Ask The Teen" on www.lovetoknow.com, and she's got the 4-1-1 on mothers and daughters.

MOM BONDING 101:

1. Dish to her. I know that sometimes "How was school?" can be the most annoying question in the universe at the end of a long, long day, but sometimes you should just humor your mom and let her in a little bit. She wants to know. Really. You don't have to give her a play-by-play of every class, but just one little anecdote about your day is better than "Fine. UGH. (doorslam)."

BRITTANY & HER MOM, TERRI

2. Let her dish to you. Okay, I know this is hard to believe, but, before Moms were Moms, they were PEOPLE. They had lives and adventures and scandalous escapades before you came along and they turned into That Woman Who Makes Your Toast. Have a pow-wow. You might be surprised.

3. Develop a secret language. You and your mom have code words for certain types of things or situations. It's a great way to get out of things you don't want to do, without hurting someone else's feelings. Let's say your friend asks you to go the movies, but you're not up for it. I used to call my mom and ask permission a certain way and she would know to say "no" and I would have good excuse to say no. Our code was "Jenny wants me to go to the movies with her, can I?" rather than "I want to go the movies with Jenny, can I?"

4. **Have some sort of food adventure.** Pick a type of food that you've never eaten before—whether its Tibetan, Brazilian, or Soul—and find a restaurant, or, if you and your mom are cooking-types, prepare some recipes, and have dinner together. You may find a new favorite food, or you may eat something horrible that traumatizes the both of you eternally—that's the adventure part! Either way it's fun, and you get to try something new.

5. **Trade favorite songs.** Make your mom a mix CD of songs you think she'd like—just remember, moms aren't typically into screamo. Then you should see if you can get her to do the same for you—who knows, you might discover some cool old people music.

Warning: doing this might actually make your mom cooler. I know, weird. You're helping her stay "with it". Think of it as good karma.

46. Have a first crush and know how to deal!

Boys on the Brain! It happens to all of us, sooner or later. 'Fess up: They can be cute, smart, fun, flirty—not to mention annoying and oh-so **CONFUSING!** Not that I'm expert (I'm only 13), but I do have some experience in the crush zone. First, I break it down into two types:

1. Shy Crush: This guy seems to be into you, but the next moment not so much! He may smile and sometimes even talk to you. Other times, he ignores you.

2. Outgoing Crush: This guy isn't afraid to show his feelings. He's always game for a convo and flashes a big 'ole smile when you pass each other in the hallway.

4 WAYS TO TELL IF YOUR CRUSH HAS A CRUSH ON YOU!

1. He always seeks you out and wants to talk.

2. When you're chatting, he leans towards you, and tries to keep eye contact.

3. He asks lots of questions about you, checking to see if you two have anything in common.

4. He will smile, and then look away from you every now and again.

NOT SURE IF YOU'RE CRUSHIN' FOR REAL? ASK YOURSELF THESE 4 QUESTIONS.

1. Does your stomach do flips and your heart start racing every time he looks your way?

2. Do you get ridiculously quiet in front of your crush (or end up doing something dorky)

3. Is your crush dominating your thoughts, even out of school?

4. Do you ever practice writing his last name as your own?

4 WAYS TO SHOW YOUR CRUSH YOU LIKE HIM:

1. Talk to him, but try not to act nervous. 'Cuz he will know something's up.

2. Whenever he's close to you, turn your head and smile! Just when his head turns to see you, quickly turn your head. This is flirting 101.

3. Be sure to make eye contact when talking to your crush.

4. Ask him about himself and his hobbies—see if you have anything in common.

Answer two or more yes, and my friend you've got a crush!

more

"The best thing to do is get to know your crush. Talk to him on the phone. Call him a few times and when he calls you back, you'll know he's interested."

—Nick Jonas

CRUSH RX: Rejection is cold, cruel, and never-deserved. Take heart: it happens to all of us! Vent with your buds, write down your feelings, take a bubble bath, or pig out—go ahead and soothe your broken heart. Just don't sulk too long! Learn to pick up the pieces and get back in the game.

47. Experiment with a **funky** hair color (not permanent, please—or your parents could lose it.)

Rock some funky hairstreaks, like Rihanna and bring out your rebel 'tude. Colorist ADRIAN WALLACE, of New York City's Rita Hazan Salon, has the 4-1-1 on creating a "TEMPORARY" yet colorful look.

1. Experiment with color without dying; by using a clip-on hair piece that snaps, rather than glues on. Look for colorful clip-on strands at costume or beauty supply stores.

2. Experiment with different colors. Fasten clips as close to scalp as possible. Strands look best if placed underneath a layer of hair, not on top or around your face.

3. Pink and fuchsia look best on light hair, while reds and blues pop on darker hair.

Being polite is way more than saying 'please' and 'thank you' (although that's important..) Good manners show respect for yourself and those around you. Etiquette expert **LEW BEYER** shares manners all polite 13-year olds should know and practice. Go ahead: Show off your social IQ.

1. BE POLITE TO YOURSELF

Show that you have self-respect by taking care of yourself; dress well, eat healthy foods, get regular exercise, and use kind words when speaking about yourself.

2. GET A GRIP

A firm handshake extended to everyone (even people your own age) sends an impression of maturity and is considered an expression of welcome and acceptance.

3. RESPECT YOUR ELDERS

Make it a habit to look adults in the eye and to address them by Mr., Miss, Ms., or Mrs. This shows that you respect authority and also that you understand that while young people can be friendly with adults, the priority for relationships between adults and young people is respect first, and friendship second.

4. BE A GRACIOUS GUEST

Try not to ever show up at an event uninvited, never come empty-handed, always offer to help or clean up, and avoid being the last to leave. Do all these things and you'll have more social invitations than you know what to do with.

5. ELBOWS OFF THE TABLE!

Any time you are eating, but especially when you are dining in a public place or are a guest at someone's home, you should keep your elbows (and sunglasses, cell phone, purse, homework, iPod, nail polish, and certainly your poodle or other pets) off the table.

6. TAKE TIME TO BE ON TIME

Being late on a regular basis tells others that you are self-absorbed or that you are disorganized.

7. BE A THOUGHTFUL GIFT GIVER

Think about how good you feel when someone takes the time to consider your wants and needs and gives a thoughtful gift (presented in pretty paper) and try to do the same for others. Avoid re-gifting and always consider how the recipient of the gift will feel when he/she receives the gift. When someone gives you a gift, show some appreciation and write a handwritten thank-you note.

8. PRACTICE GOOD POSTURE

Nothing says "I'm lazy" or "I don't care" more than slouching, dragging your feet, or sprawling when you sit. Show that you care and that you are energetic and positive by standing and sitting up straight.

9. CHOOSE PEOPLE OVER PHONES

Many people are in the habit of making the cell phone a priority and ignoring or interrupting people they are face-to-face with by talking on the phone. It is disrespectful to ask someone who is giving you his/her time to "wait a sec" while you take a call from a third party.

10. TAKE TIME TO LEARN PROPER TABLE MANNERS

Most polite people don't really care what fork you use. Still take the time to learn, and use proper table manners. It shows you understand there are social rules and want to make a good impression.

49. Know **cyber-bullying** is cruel.

Mean girls (or boys) don't just terrorize the hallways—THEY TROLL CYBERSPACE!! These nasty pests take pleasure in ruining reps, posting lies, and can make your online world a nightmare. Don't get caught in this wicked web—internet safety site www.Kidpower.com has the 4-1-1 on cyber-bullying.

DEF: Cyber-bullying is using computers, cell phones, and other technology to hurt, scare, or embarrass other people or to spread gossip or photos that will harm their reputations. It is illegal.

1. Being mean is being mean, no matter how you do it. Don't ask if it's funny. Ask if it will make someone unhappy.

Protect Yourself:
www.kidpower.org
www.stopbullyingnow.com
www.wiredkids.org

2. Even if you think someone was horrible to you, being horrible back is not a safe or ethical way to handle the problem. Instead, get help from an adult you trust.

more

3. If you get an upsetting message or see something that is attacking you: Do not reply. Do not delete. Save the message, print it if you can, and get help from an adult you trust. If one adult does not help you, keep asking until you get the help you need.

BUZZWORTHY

• 90 percent of middle schoolers polled by wiredkids.org admit to having their feelings hurt on-line.

• 75 percent of pre-teen and young teens polled by www. wiredkids.org reported being involved directly or indirectly in cyber-bullying.

MEAGHAN JETTE MARTIN

As the evil Tess, MEAGHAN JETTE MARTIN made life tough for the Camp Rock crew. But off-camera she's super-nice! And like many of us, she's had to deal with pesky Queen Bees. Here's how she survives:

• There were a group of girls in my school who were always saying nasty, rude things behind my back. It hurt! I tried hard to ignore them and not let them get in the way of my acting. I found my best friends in drama club. Common ground is a good basis for friendship.

• I am actually shy. So, I've never confronted a mean girl. But, I do think about reasons why she's treating me so bad. Have I done something? Is she going through a tough time at home? Maybe, like Tess, she's acting out because her home life isn't great. I believe in second chances, but if she keeps up her nasty ways—maybe your friendship is just not meant to be.

• I do believe if the situation gets bad, you need to seek out the advice of a trusted teacher or counselor. Teasing, social isolation, pushing, or shoving is wrong! Don't be embarrassed or afraid to seek out help.

• True friendship is based on trust. My friends and I are always happy for each other when good things happen. Jealousy is not cool!

50. Go to an amusement Park.

"Ride as many kiddie rides as you can, because when you get tall you can't go in the ball pit. Take advantage of all the rides and games at a carnival. Have fun, because when you grow up, you get busy and don't have time."

—Brittany Snow

"Go on a really scary rollercoaster and keep your hands in the air the entire time."

—Emmy Rossum

51. Ask "**why**" to everything your parents say (Obnoxious, right? But, that's us tweens for you.)

52. Learn about another **country**.

BUZZWORTHY FACTS ABOUT KIDS AROUND THE WORLD:

Cambodian kids are often given symbolic names that rhyme with one other person in the family.

It's rise and shine for students in **China**, who start classes at 7:30 a.m. School runs till 5 p.m., but kids get a two-hour lunch break. And it's not just reading, writing, arithmetic for Chinese students—they take classes in values, manners, and attitude, too.

more

Parents and kids often have different last names in **Ethiopia**. Kids usually take their dad's first name and make it their last.

School starts at 8 a.m. and goes 'till 4 p.m. in **France**, but kids get a two-hour lunch break. French schoolchildren have Wednesday and Sunday off, and have a half-day on Saturday.

Many children in **India** are expected to work! More kids have jobs to help support their families than in any other country in the world. So it's no surprise, only half of the kids finish primary school.

At mealtime in **Iran**, families gather on the floor around a tablecloth called a sofreh. Also, most Iranian children have at least one grandparent living at home with them.

School runs from April to March in **Japan**, where the six-week summer break includes homework (ew!). For Japanese students, pressure like this starts at a young age. Believe it or not, preschoolers prep for exams at "cram schools."

In **Nigeria**. older siblings get major props. As a mark of respect, an older brother or sister may be called "Senior Brother" or "Senior Sister."

Teens in **Greece** take second and third language lessons in private schools and institutes, three times a week, in the evenings. Greek schools don't offer extracurricular activities like music, art, or sports so kids do those after school too. This means many kids don't hang out with friends until the weekends.

GIRL POWER:

Inspired to help girls outside the United States? GIRLS LEARN INTERNATIONAL is one way to do it and get your friends from school involved. This nonprofit pairs groups of American middle and high-school students with a "partner classroom" in a community overseas where girls have a tough time getting an education and need help. Here's what some Girls Learn teens learned about their global sisters...

"In many African countries, such as Benin, only one girl from each village is allowed to go to school. These girls often have to travel miles through warring villages and dangerous situations just to get to school." —Jensen, 16

"Girls in India are just like girls in America; they love to play games, hang out with their friends, and they love learning. Giving them the chance to learn is one of the most rewarding things a person can do." —Emma, 15

"In many countries around the world it is difficult for girls to get an education just because they're girls." —Vanessa, 15

Have a *sleepover.*

Host a stellar slumber party. Celebrity party planner David Tutera has the tips to make it the most rockin' party ever. Remember: The best way to make friends feel at-home is to become a guest at your own party!

DO-IT-YOURSELF INVITES:

• *Send each guest a CD with some of your favorite songs.* Make a cool insert for front of case with all the party deets.

• *Make a sleep eye-mask invite.* Take two rectangles of fabric and some dried lavender or cotton. Write all the party deets on top piece with puffy painter marker. Let it set, fill, sew, and send!

MENU SUGGESTIONS:

• *Pizza is always a hit.* Order some plain cheese pies. Then, set-up a topping station with pepperoni, mushrooms, spinach, sausage, peppers—whatever.

• *Snacks are a must!* Instead of microwave popcorn, go gourmet! Serve different kinds of popcorn, like white cheddar, or chocolate and caramel drizzle. Make the ultimate "trail mix" with all your faves like flavored cereal mix, pretzels, mini marshmallows, chocolate candies, and nuts.

• *Don't forget breakfast!* Pancakes always work. But why not balance out the pig fest the night before with a smoothie station? Have an adult help you blend milk, yogurt, and favorite fruits together for a tasty treat.

ACTIVITIES:

• *Karaoke!* Keep up the energy. Karaoke machines are on the market for less than $50. Or, crank up the iPod and sing-a-long.

• *Palm Reading.* Download a chart from the internet and take turns reading each other's palm.

• *Makeover Madness:* Mani-pedis are a must (go to item #84 for more deets). Also, stock up on different makeup shades and hair accessories. Set up a face mask station. Take eveyone's pic on a digital camera, print them out, and give 'em to your guests.

• *Movies:* Make sure to have lots of girly movies on hand, like *Enchanted*, *Mean Girls*, and *Camp Rock* or watch a scary movie.

ZAP YOUR ZITS!

It's hard enough being a teen without having to worry about zits—an annoying, ugly reality for most of us. DEBI BRYNES, who had major acne as kid, now runs Clear Up Skincare, a program to help zap zits and encourage positive self-esteem, even during the nastiest breakout.

TREATMENT TIPS:

1. Don't pick at skin. Picking spreads infection and may cause permanent scarring.

2. Ice breakouts twice a day to reduce swelling and redness.

3. Don't bake your face in the sun thinking it will clear acne—it will only create more dried skin to clog the pores and result in even more breakouts.

4. Breakouts don't mean dirty skin. Avoid harsh soaps, rough washcloths, and scrubs containing nutshells—they cause irritation and worsen acne.

5. Use skin care products and makeup that are perfume free, oil free, and noncomedogenic.

6. Drink at least 8 glasses of water daily and eat leafy greens—water provides hydration and veggies help maintain good elimination.

7. Sleep 7–8 hours per night—not sleeping enough can cause physical stress, making it difficult to clear acne.

8. Avoid iodides in diet, like salty snacks, fast foods, processed foods, excessive dairy, iodized salt, and vitamins containing iodine.

9. Keep up treatment plan. Skipping home treatment allows blackheads to form deep in the follicles causing new future breakouts.

10. Use toothpaste for teeth, not blemishes—for mild acne use a topical skin care product with 2.5 percent benzoyl peroxide or salicylic acid.

11. Wash clothes and linens in perfume-free detergents and avoid fabric softeners, especially the sheets used in dryers.

12. Use glass cleaner on cell phones and all other surfaces that you hold against your skin.

13. Get plenty of exercise to help reduce stress.

More Tips: www.clearupskincare.org

"Washing your face is so important! Once, I just went to bed with my makeup on, and I completely broke out the next morning! So wash your face every morning and night."

—Emily Osment

BUZZWORTHY 85 percent of teens suffer from mild to severe acne.

55. Spin in circles 'til you feel sick.

56. Put ketchup on **everything** you eat for a day.

hotlist top 10 crazy food combos: "try em if you dare"

1. **Mayonnaise, peanut butter, and lettuce sandwich.**
2. **French fries dipped in a strawberry milkshake.**
3. **Chips, yogurt, chocolate chip cookies, and honey sandwich.**
4. **Gummy bears dipped in chocolate or vanilla icing.**
5. **Whipped cream and oranges.**
6. **Hot chocolate with Snickers and Reese's Peanut Butter Cup chunks.**
7. **Fritos dipped in peanut butter with whipped cream on top**
8. **Oreos and peanut butter. (Super Yummy!)**
9. **Extra hot grilled jalapeño dipped in melted chocolate!**
10. **A pickle between two Cheez-Its**

"You have to have a crazy binge day. A day where you eat nothing but ice cream and cookies and sit in front of the TV and watch cartoons. Just a perfect kids' day... Then go out, and do something active, like skate."

— corbin Bleu

A good 'ole tootsie rub feels great and is good for you! Reflexologists (those who rub feet for a living) believe certain areas of your feet relate to different parts of your body and by applying pressure to a specific area will heal what ails 'ya. Let's say you've got a stuffy nose: Try massaging your big toe to get rid of the discomfort. Kinda cool, huh?

REFLEXOLOGY CHART:

Apply pressure to the different points with thumb and fingers. Massage with a firm touch. Follow the chart and rub your way though all the different pressure points.

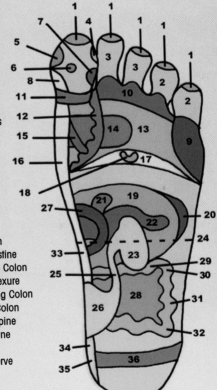

1. Brain
2. Sinuses/Outer Ear
3. Sinuses/Inner Ear/Eye
4. Temple
5. Hypothalamus
6. Pituitary
7. Side of Neck
8. Cervical Spine
9. Shoulder/Arm
10. Neck/Eye/Inner Ear
11. Neck/Thyroid/Tonsils
12. Bronchi/Thyroid
13. Chest/Lung
14. Heart
15. Esophagus
16. Thoracic Spine
17. Diaphragm
18. Solar Plexis
19. Stomach
20. Spleen
21. Adrenais
22. Pancreas
23. Kidneys
24. Waist Line
25. Ureter
26. Bladder
27. Duodenum
28. Small Intestine
29. Transverse Colon
30. Splenic Flexure
31. Descending Colon
32. Sigmoid Colon
33. Lumbar Spine
34. Sacral Spine
35. Coccyx
36. Sciatic Nerve

59. Write a 250-word **essay** and title it "All About Me!"

WRITING 101!

For some of us, writing is a snap. But if you're like most, words don't always flow. Don't panic! Remember, no essay is perfect the first go-around. My English teacher, **MS. LISA SMITH**, has these tips to jumpstart your creative juices.

MS. SMITH'S TIPS TO WRITING AN ESSAY

BRAINSTORM

• Jot down any ideas that come to your mind

• Draw on real life experiences and memorable moments

• Highlight the ideas that you want to include from your notes

OUTLINE

• Organize your ideas

• Include an introduction, at least one body paragraph and a conclusion

WRITE

• Decide which ideas will make your story strong

• Eliminate the ideas that do not support your theme

• Develop your ideas using description and details

USE YOUR VOICE

• Entertain your audience

• Make sure your personality shines through and your voice is heard

• Remember, there is no right or wrong, you are writing about you

REVISE AND EDIT

• Proofread your work

• Correct your work for any grammar, spelling or punctuation errors

BE PROUD OF YOUR WORK!

Hint: Put an away message up on IM, so friends know you're busy and you won't get distracted.

Whether it's an essay, a poem, or just your thoughts on a favorite movie or cool new tune, let your opinions be known. Blog sites are an awesome way to blurt out your thoughts and make new virtual friends. Check out:
www.newmoon.org
www.allykatzz.com

BUZZWORTHY 93 percent of teens write for their own pleasure (pew research).

60. Climb a super high tree, but be careful.

61. Learn to say "no" to **peer pressure**.

Just do it: "Say no." If your gut is telling you something is wrong, then it is! Some peeps will try and get you to cheat on a quiz, lie to your parents, skip class, or even drink alcohol—STAY STRONG—and be true to your values. Licensed Professional Counselor **SHARON SCOTT** offers these tips from her best-selling book for teens, *How to Say No and Keep Your Friends, 2nd Ed.*

• Negative peer pressure is when someone close to your age encourages you to do something that is wrong, dangerous, harmful, or illegal.

• Pay attention to how your friends talk so you will notice clues to potential trouble such as whispering or looking around to see if anyone is watching, or using pressuring lines such as "We won't get caught" or "Everyone does it."

• Don't get swayed by your friends telling you the good things that might happen. Think of the consequences such as losing privileges, a damaged reputation, and losing the respect of your parents.

• Get out of the trouble trap in 30 seconds or less by changing the subject, ("Have you seen that new guy?"), coming up with a better idea ("Let's listen to my new CD"), using flattery ("You're too smart to do that"), making a true excuse ("I've got to finish my homework"), or using any other response that screams "NO WAY."

• Peer pressure is emotional blackmail. You may worry that you'll lose friends if you don't go along with their dumb ideas. You won't ...true friends like you for who you are.

BUZZWORTHY

• 74 percent of girls say they are under pressure to please everyone.

• 87 percent of teens face at least one peer pressure situation every day.

• 62 percent of tween girls knowingly BREAK parent rules.

62. Put ice cubes down your shirt and create a *new dance*.

63. Make a *funny face* in your school picture (or just do it in the mirror).

POSE LIKE A PRO

School pics aren't life's only photo-op. There are family outings, birthdays, parties, holidays—taking pictures is a favorite tween pastime. *Access Hollywood's* NANCY O'DELL shares the scoop on how celebs maneuver their picture-perfect moves—SO YOU CAN TOO!

1. Don't wear makeup or clothes that are trendy…you will hate the picture in later years when styles go out.

2. If you are taking a group picture and want to be taller, stand closer to the camera. If you want to be shorter, stand farther away from the camera.

3. Always turn slightly sideways. A shoulders-straight-forward pose is too blunt and not as friendly.

4. Don't wear really baggy clothes or silky materials; they look sloppy in pictures.

5. And lastly—SMILE big!

64. Set off on a major **biking** adventure (and I'm not talking just 'round the hood).

BUZZWORTHY Every year over half million Americans end up in the emergency room due to a bike accident. Wearing a helmet is a must if you value your life!

65. Get a **pet** (or plant) and take care of it.

If a pet is out of the question, why not go for the green—and plant a garden? ALEX FELEPPA, director of the Horticultural Society of New York, shares a few green thumb tips to get your garden started.

1. Do your homework. You need to find the right plant for the right place. Investigate planting areas and figure out which spots are sunny and which are shady.

2. Buy both annuals and perennials. Shrubs, small trees, and ferns provide a good base, then mix it up with seasonal flowers.

3. Compost is an awesome nutrient. If it's available try mixing it into soil.

4. Know your bugs. Ladybugs and praying mantises are good. Spider mites and aphids damage plants.

5. Nurture your garden. Tend to plants at least once a week. Make sure they are getting enough sunlight and water.

66. Wear something **super scary** on Halloween

Every grownup gal knows the little black dress is a classic must-have. For us stylistas-in-training, **THE BIG BLACK T-SHIRT** is our style staple. It gets an "A" in diversity! The big black tee looks smashing worn over jeans with a leather belt or with a black skirt, a necklace, and some kickin' boots for a party look. And for our last Halloween Hoorah, crafty lady and author of *Living Artfully*, **SANDRA MAGSAMEN** shows us how to make 5 different costumes out of ONE black tee.

SKELETON

Goods You Need:

- Big black tee
- White acrylic paint
- Black leggings

To Make:
Print out a pic of a skeleton for inspiration (or trace outline on shirt), and paint bones with white paint. Wear with leggings.

WITCH

Goods You Need:

- Black tee
- Marabou
- Hot glue gun
- A witch hat
- Striped leggings

To Make:
Simply glue marabou to neckline, on cuffs and around hem of t-shirt. Wear with a black hat and tights.

CAT

Goods You Need:

- Black tee
- Marabou
- Hot glue gun
- Headband
- Leggings

To Make:
Glue marabou to headband to make ears. Glue marabou to neckline, on cuffs, around the hem of t-shirt, and on back of t-shirt to make a purrfect tail. Wear with leggings.

BUMBLE BEE

Goods You Need:

- Black tee
- Black pipe cleaners
- Yellow felt
- Hot glue gun
- Bee wings (buy at costume store)
- Black leggings

To Make:
Glue black pipe cleaners to headband to make antennae, glue strips of yellow felt around t-shirt to form bee body, add bee wings, and get buzzing. Don't forget the leggings!

ROCK STAR

Goods You Need::

- Black tee
- Acrylic paint
- Belt
- Lots of jewels
- Striped leggings

To Make:
Paint a cool design on t-shirt with acrylic paint, and add a belt. Accessorize with lots of jewelry and wear colored leggings to make a superstar outfit.

Make a **friendship bracelet** for your BFF.

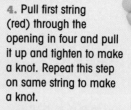

Swap friendship bracelets with your best bud. Have her make a wish when you tie it around her wrist, and when the bracelet falls off the wish will come true.

THINGS YOU NEED:
- **Different colors of embroidery thread (more string = wider bracelet).**
- **Scissors**
- **Cardboard**
- **Tape**

1. Wrap a string around wrist 2 times to find right length. Cut a piece this long from each of the colors. 8 – 10 strings work best for a bracelet.

2. Hold the ends of all the strings together (about 1" from the top) and make a knot. Tape a knot to cardboard.

3. Cross far left string (red) over the string to the right (green), creating a shape like the #4.

4. Pull first string (red) through the opening in four and pull it up and tighten to make a knot. Repeat this step on same string to make a knot.

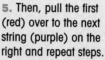

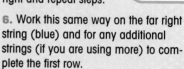

5. Then, pull the first (red) over to the next string (purple) on the right and repeat steps.

6. Work this same way on the far right string (blue) and for any additional strings (if you are using more) to complete the first row.

7. Start next row using the string to the far left. Repeat all the same steps until you have a row finished.

8. Keep going until bracelet is long enough to fit around wrist. Tie the loose ends of your fitted bracelet with a square knot (just how you started). Be sure there's enough string left over to tie an end knot and secure onto friend's wrist.

TO CAMP ROCK'S ALYSON STONER, A GOOD FRIEND IS...

A Unique individual— Everyone is an individual, but those who conform to gain popularity aren't being true to themselves. Someone who's comfortable in their own skin won't compete with you or reveal your insecurities to raise themselves.

A Good Listener—People who truly listen to your feelings understand that it's not always about them and are willing to help at any given moment.

Responsible—People who manage their time properly and stay on track are positive influences for us. Plus, they'll score parental approval easily!

Flexible—Friendships aren't rigid. If it feels like there's a written document controlling what you can and cannot do, then you won't grow, change, and make new friends like you're supposed to. Make sure your good friend allots you some freedom!

68. Go off the *high dive* even if you don't dive.

69. Make dinner for your **parents**.

KATIE LEE JOEL's love of cooking goes way back to her childhood. Now, the lifelong foodie and author of *Comfort Food* shares a few simple (but tasty) recipes all aspiring young cooks can whip up.

TURKEY MEATLOAF

2 pounds ground turkey

½ medium onion, grated

½ teaspoon thyme

¾ cup ketchup, divided

½ cup dried bread crumbs

1 large egg, lightly beaten

½ teaspoon salt

¼ teaspoon black pepper

Preheat oven to 400 F.

In a large bowl, combine turkey, onion, thyme, ½ cup ketchup, bread crumbs, egg, salt, and pepper. Using your hands, gently mix until all the ingredients are combined.

Place meat mixture onto a baking sheet lined with parchment paper or aluminum foil. Shape the meat into a loaf about 9 inches long and 4 inches wide. Top with remaining ¼ cup ketchup. Bake 45–50 minutes. Let stand 10 minutes before slicing.

SIMPLE GREEN SALAD WITH CLASSIC VINAIGRETTE

1 head lettuce (romaine, bibb, iceberg, etc)

3 tablespoons extra virgin olive oil

2 tablespoons red wine vinegar

1 teaspoon Dijon mustard

1 shallot, minced

½ teaspoon salt

¼ teaspoon black pepper

Extras: **sliced cucumber, shredded carrots, diced tomatoes, etc.**

Combine lettuce and any extra vegetables in a medium bowl. In a glass jar or plastic container with a tight-fitting lid, combine the oil, vinegar, mustard, shallot, salt, and pepper. Shake to combine. Pour over salad and toss. Serve immediately.

BEST CHOCOLATE-CHIP COOKIES

2 ¼ cups all-purpose flour

¾ teaspoon baking soda

1 teaspoon baking powder

1 teaspoon salt

8 tablespoons (1 stick) unsalted butter, at room temperature

2/3 cup packed brown sugar

1 cup granulated sugar

2 large eggs

1 teaspoon pure vanilla extract

1 (12 ounce) bag semi-sweet chocolate chips

Preheat oven to 375 degrees F. Position a rack in the middle of the oven. Grease two cookie sheets.

In a medium bowl, mix flour, baking soda, baking powder, and salt.

In a large bowl, using an electric mixer, cream the butter and sugars, until light and fluffy, about 3 minutes. Add the eggs, one at a time, beating until incorporated. Beat in the vanilla. Mix in the dry ingredients with the mixer on low speed until just combined. Stir in the chocolate chips.

Scoop by the heaping tablespoonful onto the cookie sheets. Bake until golden and chewy, about 12–15 minutes. Transfer the cookies to a rack to cool. Store in an airtight container.

70. Have a signature **scent**.

Every gal needs a special scent (or two)! Research shows different aromas trigger different moods and memories. So, to play up your many-many sides, Coty fragrance guru Lori Singer suggests every young teen have a "wardrobe of fragrance." Here's her take on basic scents-ability.

Girly:

You're feeling playful 'n flirty. A fruity-floral mix of vanilla, Tahitian tiare flower, and golden apricot will enhance your bubbly mood. It's a subtle shout-out you're super sweet, but also really fun.

Pick: Vera Wang Princess

Sassy:

You've got a party on the social agenda and you're game to steal the spotlight and get noticed! Flaunt your rebel 'tude with a sweet 'n spicy combo of sleek woods, sparkling pear, and sweat pea. It's the scent of a gal who's confident, and ready to take the dare.

Pick: Harajuku Lovers 'Music' by Gwen Stefani

Free-Spirited:

Got a picnic planned with your buds and word has it your crush may drop by. Make a lasting impression with a burst of sunshine scents like wild strawberry, violet, and white wood. Let your easy-going earth-girl spirit linger on his mind.

Pick: Daisy by Marc Jacobs

Spunky:

Need to round up the troops and get your buds to vote you in as class prez or back your campaign to get healthier foods on the cafeteria menu? Go for a subtle scent that commands leadership, but doesn't overpower you (or your mission). Try a clean n' spirited smell of papaya, bergamot, and musk— and the power of persuasion is yours.

Pick: ck one

"Making a fragrance is different in a way because it's so abstract. You really can't put your finger on it; you have to put your nose on it, which makes it fun. I guess it's similar to music because when you are creating it you have to find the words to describe it—which can be difficult."

— Gwen Stefani

71. Learn to say "*I love you*" in different languages.

PASS ON THE
MESSAGE OF LOVE
WORLDWIDE.

Indonesian:
Saya cinta kamu

French:
Je t'aime

Turkish:
Seni seviyorum

Mandarin Chinese:
Wo ai ni

Spanish:
Te amo

Italian:
Ti amo

Write a **fan letter** to your fave star.

SAY "HI" TO YOUR FAVORITE CELEB:

ALY & AJ
c/o Hollywood Records
500 S. Buena Vista St.
Burbank, CA 91521

BRITTANY & ZAC EFRON

more

MILEY CYRUS
c/o The Disney Channel
4401 Sunset Blvd.
Burbank, CA 91505

ZAC EFRON
P.O. Box 960
Avila Beach, CA 93424

GOSSIP GIRL CAST
c/o The CW
3300 W. Olive Ave.
Burbank, CA 91505

DEMI LOVATO
c/o The Disney Channel
3800 Alameda Ave.
Burbank, CA 91505

**WIZARDS OF
WAVERLY PLACE**
c/o The Disney Channel
3800 Alameda Ave.
Burbank, CA 91505

JONAS BROTHERS
c/o Hollywood Records
500 S. Buena Vista St.
Burbank, CA 91521

RIHANNA
c/o Island Def Jam Records
825 Eight Ave.
New York, Ny 10019

BRITTANY &
JONAS BROTHERS

73. IM your **BFF** for at least 2 hours (or go old school and chat on the phone).

Girl Code: The language of a new generation.

Examples:

LUSM: love you so much
WE: whatever
IMO: in my opinion
TTYS: talk to you soon
BFFL: best friend for life
G2G: got to go
SWAK: sealed with a kiss
BRB: be right back
PAL: parents are listening
BRT: be right there

IMU: I miss you
SYS: see you, soon
TCOY: take care of yourself
SPST: same place, same time
EOM: end of message
JW: just wondering
CUZ: because
WB: write back
POS: parents over shoulder
JK: just kidding
P911: parent alert

4-1-1 Beware of frenemies. YOU know the girl who pretends to be your friend, but really isn't. She'll spill your secrets, doesn't have your back, and everything is always about her. Cut the ties, 'cuz you will get hurt.

74. Put fake tattoos all over your body.

75. **Sing** out loud.

13 is such an awesome age! Even Broadway put on a show just about us—"13 The Musical." It spotlights all our drama: friends, rumors, cliques, parents, kids of divorce—it's right in tune with our teen spirit. And for those of us who dream of being the next Julia Roberts or just want to pass drama class, here's some Acting 101 from a few of the show's teen stars.

BREAKING INTO THE BIZ:

"Get involved in reputable community theaters. Try different ones so you get to work with and learn from different directors. Even if you don't get the part you want don't give up. The friends you make and the commitment to this "sport" are worth the time.

—Allie Trim

DON'T LET STAGE FRIGHT BRING YOU (OR YOUR GRADE) DOWN:

"If you are scared you don't know your lines before a performance, don't fret, just concentrate on giving it your best try. It is better to focus 100 percent on your performance and mess up a few words (who cares)."

— Graham Phillips

PREP TO BE YOUR BEST:

"My best advice is to warm up your voice with breathing and vocal exercises; as well as a physical warm up to get your body stretched and ready to go. Drinking lots of water and staying away from dairy products will also help your vocals."

— Delaney Moro

ACTING BOOSTS CONFIDENCE:

"I am really very shy; I spend most of my time reading, writing stories and poems. When I'm onstage I become someone else. This helps me become more outgoing and social in my off-stage life, too.

— Caitlin Gann

76. Run, jump, slip, and slide! Fly down a *slip-and-slide* ten times in a row.

77. Play a **team** sport.

BE SPORTY.

Expert after expert will tell you: Sports do a body (and mind) good. They make you stronger, more flexible, improve coordination, reduce stress, energize you, and boost your brain power—the list goes on and on. Olympic Gold medalist Brandi Chastain, who played on the U.S. Women's soccer team, shares how sports helped her develop lifelong skills—that go way beyond the playing field.

Learn dedication. And, that's what you should want in anything in life—whether it's sports, school, or your job.

Learn respect. Every player (no matter their position or skill level) has significance on the game's outcome.

Learn to get along. To be a successful team player you need to communicate, be a good listener, and be accepting of different personalities.

Learn goal-setting. To be a good athlete, you need to practice and keep at it. I used to write down the parts of my game I wanted to improve and tape the list in places I would see everyday—like the inside of my locker.

Learn that things don't always go your way. Whether through injuries or making a lousy play, I learned to look at my effort and improve. Everybody makes mistakes. Don't be afraid to push yourself! If there's no risk, there's no gain.

Learn to enjoy. When you enjoy yourself, you'll learn, you'll want more information, and you'll push yourself.

"I tried every sport in high school, or just growing up. I think it makes your school experience and memories just so much better."

—Blake Lively

78. Learn about your family **history**.

Think Miley Cyrus may be your long-lost cousin or your ancestors are the Rockefellers? Discover your roots. The easiest way to get started is to interview your relatives and map out a family tree. See how many gens you can go back. Want to dig deeper? Branch out via the web. ALERT: Some of these sites will cost 'ya, so get your parent's ok.

Family Roots:
www.ancestory.com
www.familysearch.org
www.genealogybank.com

79. Eat in dinner in reverse: Start with dessert, then your entrée, and finish with an appetizer.

80. Appreciate **Art**.

Art is s-o-o-o much more than a pic on a canvas. Be inspired. Be curious. Be motivated to learn more. WITT SIASOCO heads up a program at the Walker Art Center in Minneapolis, which teaches teens, and now YOU, to take a second look.

1. Take a good look.
What do you notice? What colors did the artist use? What materials did they use? What is the most striking feature of the artwork?

2. Don't be afraid to ask questions.
Find the nearest person and ask them questions about the artwork. As a person that works a museum, I know that the people that work here love to talk about art, so make sure to put them to work.

3. Step into the artist's world.
Place yourself in the artist's shoes and try to think about the artwork from their perspective. What do you think they were trying to communicate?

more

4. Form a meaning of your own.

What does this artwork remind you of and how do you feel when you look at the art? There are plenty of experts out there, but the best way to look at art is to form a meaning of your own. Most people think that there are right or wrong answers when looking at art, but your opinion is just as valid as anyone else's.

5. Have your own opinion and voice it.

Art is no fun if people don't interact and talk about it, so make sure to talk about the art. Once you have formed a meaning of your own, then voice your opinion to spark conversation with your friends.

6. Find out more about the art.

Just because you leave the artwork doesn't mean you need to stop thinking about it. To have a better understanding of the art, try to get all of the lingering questions that you had when you left the artwork answered. Can you say Google?

7. Make an artwork of your own.

Sometimes what may look easy might not be as it seems. Go home and try to reproduce an artwork that you just looked at and start a conversation with your friends about your own artwork!

---

81. Lay out in a *kiddie pool* on a really hot day.

BUZZWORTHY Sun protection is no joke. Most skin cancer is caused by sun damage that happened before the age of 20.

82. Sign up to be the **leader** of a club or captain of a sports team.

Do you want be the first female president or the head of a major company? Well, you can! First learn to be a leader now—so you can make a big difference in the world later! **DAWN NOCERA** is the force behind www.EducatingJane.com, a Web site dedicated to motivating and inspiring girls just like us!

DAWN'S 8 LITTLE LEADERSHIP TIPS

1. Make others feel important. **When your friends and the people you come into contact with feel that you recognize their strengths and contributions, they will be more willing to take note of yours.**

2. Have a clear vision of what you want done and be enthusiastic about promoting it. **People like to know what they are supposed to be doing and why. They will be more willing to assist you if you show them the value in what they are doing.**

3. Treat others the way you want to be treated. **The golden rule is timeless. Good leaders are good to their people and do not hold onto double standards.**

4. Admit when you have made a mistake. **It is always better to admit a mistake than to lose credibility by letting someone else find out about it later. Do this openly, honestly, and as soon as possible.**

more

5. Praise in public and offer constructive criticism in private. When someone has done something wrong, it's always best to correct them away from the group, so you don't embarrass anyone. If they've done a great job, tell everyone all about it. Making others feel good inspires them to work harder and get the job done.

6. Be visible. Make appearances. Everyone knows them because they make an effort to get to know everyone. You don't have to do this in a showy way, just get out there and get to know as many people as you can.

7. Strive to be the best you can be. Be coachable. That means being open to constructive criticism and making corrections as needed. Great leaders learn as much as they can about themselves and re-evaluate their leadership skills after every project. What worked? What didn't work? How can I lead better next time?

Take Charge! Read more...
www.educatingjane.com

GIRL POWER:

"Leaders are able to make good decisions for the group, not just for themselves." —Nicole, 12, Florida

"A leader needs to be open to ideas, kind, encouraging, supportive, and loves to help others." —Victoria, 13, Massachusetts

"The hardest skill to develop as a leader is learning to stand up for yourself and act on your ideas. Having people follow you will come, you first need to show them that you have a good idea and you are acting on it." —Hannah, 14, Massachusetts

83. Eat sour candy (or lemons) and see how many it takes before you have to make a funny face.

84. **Shave** your legs.

SHAGGY LEGS! HAIRY PITS! IT'S TOUGH TO FEEL CUTE IF YOU'RE FEELING SCARY HAIRY. MAYBE IT'S TIME TO BREAK OUT THE RAZOR. BEFORE YOU DO, GET YOUR PARENTS OK AND LEARN HOW TO DE-HAIR WITH CARE.

"I begged my mom to let me shave my legs. She finally let me when I turned 13."

– Molly Simms

- Never use a dull razor. (Blades should be changed every 4 – 6 uses.)

- Best time to shave is after a shower. Some gals like to do it in the shower.

- Dampen legs. Lather up shaving cream, one leg at time.

- Start at your ankle and gently pull razor upwards (in opposite direction of hair growth). Be extra careful around your knees, shins, and ankles (bony areas are easier to cut).

- Keep shaving until hair is gone; then repeat on other leg.

- Be sure to moisturize after shaving!

Tip: If you run out of shaving cream, hair conditioner can be an awesome substitute.

Ditch the little girl vibe! It's time to update your room and go for something a little more grown-up and HIP! After all, there's no space more important than your bedroom. It's where you do homework, chat with friends, hide from pesky sibs, or look in the mirror trying on outfit after outfit 'til you score the right one. So, what if you can't afford to buy all new furniture? Interior decorator REBECCA COLE has lots of ways to jazz up your room without going broke. Remember the 3 C's: Comfy, Crafty, and Cost-effective.

LOTS & LOTS OF PICS:

Framed pics of you, your buds, your family, even your celebrity crush declares this space is yours.

PAINT YOUR ROOM:

Color is a great mood changer. Paint your wall color in a single bold color like hot pink, canary yellow, or tangerine orange. Too many crazy colors in one room can look like confusion or mud! Flip thru a DIY book and be inspired to stencil your walls.

DIY ACCESSORIES:

Be inspired by crafty projects in decorating mags. There are tons of awesome rainy day projects. Add a hipster glow to your room by wrapping a colorful scarf around the drum shade of a lamp and clip the lose ends on the top and bottom with office or hair clips.

MIX 'N MATCH LINENS:

Nix the princess sheets. Instead, experiment with bold-colored stripes and floral, solids and texture, and mix the pillowcases with a different duvet. Matching is so passé!

MULTITASKING FURNITURE:

If you're going to splurge on new furniture, look for pieces that do double duty. Think: Cubes that store things, but also serve as a seat or footrest, an armoire that opens up into a desk. Or a foldup bed that is both an ottoman and a second bed for sleepovers.

Paint each of your toenails a **different** color, and flaunt 'em.

Invite your pals over for a pedi-party. Have everyone bring a different color polish and share the goods. Treat your feet to a rainbow of color.

DASHING DIVA HAS THE RECIPE FOR A SOLE SOOTHING AT-HOME PEDI.

#1 SOAK & SOFTEN: Soak feet in warm soapy water for a few minutes. Add a few of drops of your favorite essential oil (i.e. lavender to chill or lemon to energize).

#2 EXFOLIATE: First, file to smooth out rough edges. Wet legs to knee and apply your fave scrub (or use recipe below). Rub and rinse. Leaves feet silky smooth.

#3 MOISTURIZE: Dry legs and slather on your fave lotion.

#4 PREP: Using acetone or other nail polish remover, clean the whole toenail plate. This is to get rid of any lotion, so polish will adhere.

#5 POLISH: Go wild with color!

BONUS FEET TREAT: (DIY YUMMY SOAK FROM BLISS SPA)

HOT MILK & ALMOND SOAK; (SEE STEP #1) Heat up half a gallon of whole milk and combine with a little warm water. Add few drops of almond extract. While the milk is heating, in separate bowl, combine salt (coarse is best) and some type of oil (from kitchen) to make a rough paste. This can be used later as an exfoliating scrub. When heated (not boiling—make sure it's a comfy temp), empty milk into large tub (big enuf for both of your feet) and soak your tootsies.

87. Fly a kite.

88. Send a secret Valentine to your **crush**.

Let out your crushin' feelings in a poem or a song. You don't ever need to send it, just be inspired by your cutie. New York City songwriter and performer **MARY JENNINGS** is a mentor for a young lady your age at NYC's Girls Quest, a youth services agency for girls, and she offers some great ideas below:

"I think it's always cute when a girl writes me letters or something like that. Letters are always cool."

–Joe Jonas

MARY'S TIPS:

• **Be honest.** You can always be poetic and romantic without being over-dramatic and overwhelming. You never want to scare them off!

• **If you don't understand it, your crush won't understand it.** Make sure that you use language that makes sense to you. There is no need to use more complicated language than necessary. You are trying to send a message of love, not confuse them.

• **Be willing to break the rules of standard poetry.** Don't feel like you have to rhyme or stay within a particular pattern. Some of the best poets in history have broken these rules.

• **Be ready for any response that you will receive from your work and accept it gracefully.** Know that not everyone will like what you have written, but it is beautiful and wonderful because it is part of you.

• **Keep a copy for yourself.** Even though this poem or song may be for someone else, it is still your creation and you may want to look at it later on.

So is astrology for real? We don't know—but it's definitely tonsa fun! Astro gal KELLY WHITE put together some "psychic" predictions. She looked into her crystal ball and found out which celebrities would make your most astro-rific BFF and zodiac-fab crush. Starry-eyed?

Aries 3/21- 4/20

Ah, the luck of the Aries girl ...but make no mistake, not everything is left to chance. You're full-on in charge, Ramsie, and you often have a flock of followers. But you know for sure which friends are true-blue. Or do you? It's great to trust, but no buddy, er, nobody has your back like you do. Complement your competence by rocking your self-confidence! (Now, say that 10 times fast.)

Cosmic Celeb BFF: Gemini *Natalie Portman* (June 9) She's one-of-a-kind. Correction: The Twin is twice as nice ....Or is it double trouble?

Star Struck Crush: Sagittarius *Cody Linley* (November 20) This one's an adventure guy—and cute to boot—so sign up for the excitement plan!

Taurus 4/21-5/21

Taurus girl, you are sooo stubborn. But that's what makes you lovingly loyal. Heck, you have bushels of stand-up qualities: integrity, determination, warmth ...we don't have room to list them all. But our favorite trait is how you always point out the sunny side of a sitch and, even better, you look past your friends' flaws to shine all over their strengths. And that's no Bull!

Cosmic Celeb BFF: Pisces *Emily Osment* (March 10) The Fish swims in dreamy waters, so you two share a sense of whimsy ... and humor. Sleepover!

Star Struck Crush: Capricorn *Orlando Bloom* (January 13) You know full well he's too old for you in real life, but you tend to go for the mature types.

more

Gemini 5/22-6/21

Hey, Gem, wanna chat? Yeah, you do! You have the gift of gab. Or is it a curse? You tell it like it is, and people either love it or hate it. And guess what—you couldn't care less either way. What they see is what they get, right? Truth is, even your frenemies are secretly intrigued by your magnetic persona. You have 'em twice as mesmerized, Twin girl!

Cosmic Celeb BFF: Aquarius *Emma Roberts* (February 10) The girl can be as serious as a heart murmur...but what a serious sweetheart!

Star Struck Crush: Leo *Joe Jonas* (August 15) ...Talk about heart-throb! This luscious Lion is a triple threat: cute, charming and musically inclined.

Cancer 6/22-7/23

Some call you the moon maiden, Cancer chica, but we say you're a mood goddess. Your emotions tend to swing like a lead pendant on a silver chain, but your level of passion can be inspiring. Except, of course, when your Crab claws come out. Yet there's never a dull moment, and your intentions are always good. Everyone in your crew knows you as the gal who really 'n' truly cares. So there!

Cosmic Celeb BFF: Scorpio *Adrienne Bailon* (October 24) If anyone can coax you out of your shell, it's a Scorp. The party's just begun!

Star Struck Crush: Pisces *Corbin Bleu* (February 21) He's got it all—talent, charisma, happenin' hair. To sum it up in one word: dreamy!

Leo 7/24-8/23

We're not lyin', Lion, when we say you were born under one of the most dynamic signs of the zodiac. You're the leader of your pack, and you have such a BIG heart and tonsa courage. No, we're not deliberately alluding to Oz but ...you could never get lost in a poppy field because you're the girl in sizzling purple satin or the one with the most uppity up 'do. You like to make a statement, but no need to say a word—they'll hear ya roar!

Cosmic Celeb BFF: Aries *Kristen Stewart* (April 9) The Ram is a leader, and so are you. Hey, looks like you've met your match!

Star Struck Crush: Libra *Zac Efron* (October 18) What's not to love about this lovely Libra of a boy? Yum. Need we say more?

Virgo 8/24-9/23

Brittany & Penn Badgley

You appear to be so squeaky clean and pristine, Virgo girl, all put together even under extreme pressure. But c'mon admit it—beneath that sparkling veneer, you're slightly disheveled on the inside. People would be surprised to know you're not the picture of ultimate excellence—anyway, who is? And besides, you're pretty darn close. You're a smart cookie, so learn this: It's OK to be off-kilter at times as long as you keep it real!

Cosmic Celeb BFF: Capricorn *Jordin Sparks* (December 22) This Capricorn gal is solid, like you! Dependable, driven and rock-steady.

Star Struck Crush: Scorpio *Penn Badgley* (November 1) It's not his dark-side aura that attracts you. It's his debate-club demeanor.

Libra 9/24-10/23

Libra gal, your specialty is pulling off the best-ever balancing routine. You take a good long look at an issue from every possible angle before standing firmly behind an opinion. Once you've made up your mind, you're not so easily swayed. But no matter which side of the bleachers you're sitting on, you're the girl who cultivates harmony between the opposing teams. Peace out!

Cosmic Celeb BFF: Leo *Demi Lovato* (August 20) She's outgoing, easy-going and going...to always be there for you! Loyal, this one.

Star Struck Crush: Gemini *Shia LaBeouf* (June 11) You love to entertain, and this action-loving cutie is a people person, too. With a solid social life in the mix, you two will never be bored.

Scorpio 10/24-11/22

Scorpio sister, some see you as shy and reclusive. And you can be. But you also love to bust out and embrace your inner wild child! This unpredictable nature of yours lends an air of mystery, and that's why peeps are often puzzled. Keep 'em guessing, Scorp. But make sure they get this message loud and clear: You are NOT interested in the superficial. Insincere friends need not apply.

Cosmic Celeb BFF: Cancer *Selena Gomez* (July 22) You two could have fun, fun, fun forever and ever and ever and ever and...

Star Struck Crush: Virgo *Nick Jonas* (September 16) He's soft-spoken, while you're outspoken. Consider it a complement!

more

Sagittarius 11/23-12/21

Archer girl, you're right on target. You know what you want and exactly how to go for it! The best part is that you're a straight shooter, Sag. You don't pretend to be somebody you aren't, not even for your crush. If he doesn't like you just the way you are, no biggie. Who needs him? Tons of people love everything that makes you ...unique!

Cosmic Celeb BFF: Libra *Hilary Duff* (September 28) Some underestimate her smarts, but no one can argue this: She'll love ya like a sister!

Star Struck Crush: Aquarius *Ricky Ullman* (January 24) You really go for that boy-next-door stuff. You guys could chat it up for hours!

Capricorn 12/22-1/20

You're happy, Cappy, and a little flirty too! Boys like that. But girls gravitate to you, as well, so you probably have a pretty well-rounded posse. With your mad social skills, you'd make a righteous contender in the school election. And you know who else gives you a thumbs-up? Teachers, of all people! You get an A+ in conscientiousness, even if you misspelled it on the pop quiz. Capricorn for class prez!

Cosmic Celeb BFF: Virgo *Blake Lively* (August 25) You have total respect for The Virg! She sooo rocks it confident—hot on the social scene.

Star Struck Crush: Taurus *Robert Pattinson* (May 13) Hey, it's like magic. This guy is a little mysterious and loads of fun!

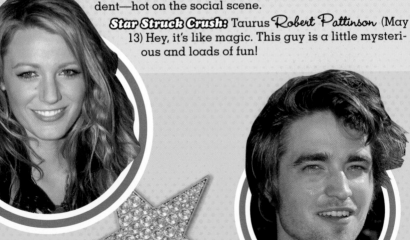

Aquarius 1/21-2/19

You have an analytical mind, Miss Aquarius. You're super-smart and like to pick things apart. Still, you appreciate all things creative and artistic. But if you take up an interest, say in ballet, you might study and dissect the joy right out of it. Keep it chill, air-sign sister. Like you do when you're kickin' it around with your best guy friend.

Cosmic Celeb B.F.F.: Sagittarius Vanessa Hudgens (December 14) The Sag's creative, spontaneous nature totally appeals to you. Right?

Star Struck Crush: Aries Jesse McCartney (April 9) A girl can fantasize (ew, the goose pimples), but the Aries boy rarely sticks to just one girl.

Pisces 2/20-3/20

You have a sentimental soul, pretty Pisces. Of all the signs, you're the one who has the most vivid imagination. But you often get frustrated when your save-the-world fantasies don't turn into reality. Break too-big ambitions into do-able goals, and you'll soon find that every little bit makes a diff. You might even figure out that dreams really do come true...

Cosmic Celeb B.F.F.: Taurus Miranda Cosgrove (May 14) You both have a love of Mama Nature. It makes for a truly beautiful friendship....

Star Struck Crush: Cancer Chace Crawford (July 18) Sure, he's cute. But he also has that certain je-ne-sais-quoi. Ooh-la-la.

Brittany & Chace Crawford

90. *Jump* off a swing in mid-air.

91. Nail a perfect 10.

Give yourself a great mani! MICHELE PIERNO of Kiss nail products knows how to hang 10.

HINTS: PLACE A PAPER TOWEL OVER WORK AREA TO PROTECT FURNITURE SURFACE!

Begin with dominant hand first — if you are right-handed, trim and file your right hand first. (Same goes for applying polish and you won't feel so clumsy when you do the opposite hand!)

STUFF YOU NEED:
- Cotton pads
- Polish remover – acetone-based
- Manicure stick
- Cotton swab
- Nail file – medium fine grit
- Soft white buff block – extra fine grit
- Cuticle oil
- Base coat
- Nail polish color
- Topcoat

DIY MANI:

1. Remove old polish with a cotton ball. Wipe downward so no polish gets on fingers and skin.

2. File and shape nails. Avoid filing into sides of nails, which can weaken them. File in only one direction, not back and forth, or nails could split and tear.

3. Lightly buff the surface nail with a soft, fine grit buff block to remove ridges, stains on nails, and excess skin that grows near the cuticle.

4. Apply cuticle oil. (Olive oil works great as cuticle oil!)

5. Gently push back cuticles with a manicure stick.

6. Wash hands in soapy water.

7. Apply one even layer of base coat. Let dry.

8. Apply polish. Start with one strip of polish down the center of nail, then swipe brush on the left and right sides. Do two thin coats. Let dry.

9. Finish with a topcoat. It helps prevents chips and makes nails shiny.

92. Do an at-home science experiment.

The Girlstart group offers a few fun (and sometimes messy) ways to explore the science around you!

1. Meltdown: **Take your two favorite shades of lipstick and melt them together to make a new shade!**

2. Design Challenge: **Host a fashion "dye off" and see who can make the most unique creation. Use bleach, dyes, or paint to create your own couture.**

3. Mix it up: **See what happens when you mix a can of soda with a box of your mom's cake mix.**

4. Ask Why: **You know how little kids always ask "why?" Try it for a few days and see if you learn something new!**

93. **Finish** the monkey bars without your feet touching the ground.

Be nice to the kid who is *left out*
(mean girls are so not cool).

DON'T LET A MEAN GIRL BRING YOU DOWN!

The truth is, every grade's got at least one. Most of us (your fave stars included) gotta deal with a mean girl at some point. Teasing, spreading rumors, or keeping you off the invite list are a few of her nasty tactics. Don't let this mastermind of misery ruin your life. *Twilight* co-stars ASHLEY GREENE and RACHELLE LEFEVRE, who both survived a school meanie, know how to take the sting out of the Queen Bee.

ASHLEY

The Toxic Times:

"I went to a new school in 6th grade and the "popular" girl turned everyone against me because I wouldn't stop dating a guy she liked. I also had someone start a rumor that I paid people to vote for me when I got middle school princess."

–Ashley

RACHELLE

"I was the kid who often ate lunch alone and I was rarely invited to the 'cool' parties. When I finally worked up the courage to go the 7th grade dance, a mean girl ruined my rep by starting a rumor I kissed seven guys that night. The next school day, my locker got peppered with horrible notes."

– Rachelle

Survival Skills:

"I was obsessed with being popular. At thirteen, I realized the "popular" kids were a very small group and I was missing out on the chance to make true friends. Also, by not letting others dictate my actions, I learned to be independent and like myself for who I am."

– Rachelle

"At times I thought my world was going to end from all the rumors! I dealt with my mean girl head on. Confronting someone doesn't have to be aggressive. Once my mean girl and I understood and reasoned with each other, we actually became civil."

–Ashley

Be You:

"If you aren't part of the popular clique… so what? Sometimes that's not the best place to be. Find people who share your similar interests and make you happy. I love goofing off with my girl or guy friends and not have to worry about what they will think, even if I am a nerd sometimes."

– Ashley

"I broke out of 'my need to popular' by developing other passions. I joined the soccer team, the drama club, and the student council. Not only did my confidence improve, but also since I was busy (and not fixated on being popular) the kids who used to torment me stopped. The 'cool" kids never invited me to their parties, but in 11th grade I was their class president."

– Rachelle

more

Keep cool: Next time Little Miss Witch tries to upset you, hold your own, but don't go into attack mode. Speak clearly and concisely so you show her you're not so easy to walk over.

Move on: At some point, a mean girl will move on to a new target. And you should move on too, by not drowning in negative feelings toward her. Feel sorry for her, because she's gotta be really insecure to tear people down to make herself feel better.

Send a SOS: There's a difference between a mean girl and an all-out bully. If you feel threatened, anxious, or just unable to function as your normally fun self, it's time to ask for help.

95.   Master a magic trick.

CRISS ANGEL shares his favorite: The Vanishing Toothpick. All you need is a toothpick and a piece of tape.

To prep—simply, fashion a piece of tape into a cone shape and stick it to the back of your left thumbnail (the opening to face the bottom of the appendage).

Casually take a toothpick from your mouth and tell your audience you will miraculously make the toothpick disappear.

Put the toothpick in the cone-shaped vise located on the back of your thumb and then clasp it down with the forefinger of your left hand. This will make the toothpick stay in place during the trick.

The toothpick is now in full view of your audience.

Next, simply flick your thumb upwards and open your fist. The toothpick should stay glued to the cone-shaped piece of tape on your nail and subsequently appear to have astonishingly vanished. (Try adding a snap of the forefinger and thumb of your right hand as you flick your left thumb upwards)

Check out more cool tricks in the book *Mindfreak: Secret Revelations* or the Master Mindfreaks DVD Series on www. CrissAngel.com

To bring it back simply return the left thumb and left forefinger to their original position.

96. **Floss** your teeth.

97. Be money **smart**.

It's great to earn extra cash babysitting or at an afterschool job, but don't rush to the mall and spend it all! Before you buy, ask yourself, "Do I really need this?". Financial guru and *Today Show's* money expert JEAN CHATZKY shares her 2 cents on money smarts so we can use our money NOW and LATER.

SPEND WISELY:

• There is a lot of stuff we want, but there are very few things that we need. Food, water, shelter top the list of things we need, while designer clothes, iPods, and fancy cell phones don't! This doesn't mean you can't buy the things you want, it's just that your needs come first. Then slowly save up to buy the extras.

• Waiting to spend comes with huge rewards. For one, if you put your money in a savings account that earns interest, it will grow (if you spend it, it's gone). If you wait to buy something you want, you might decide that you can live without it, and then you'll have money saved to spend on something you REALLY want. It's always better to sleep on a purchase than to make an impulse buy.

BE SMART AND BUDGET:

• If you have money, divide it equally into 3 piles: Save, Spend, and Donate.

• Put the Save pile in the bank, and use the Spend to go to the movies or buy things you want. Then, pick a cause you care about and with the help of your parents—it can be your church, a school group, or any organization that interests you—and give money from the Donate pile on a regular basis. YOU'RE NEVER TOO YOUNG OR EARN TOO LITTLE TO GIVE BACK!

LEARN TO GROW YOUR MONEY:

• Want to invest for the long haul? Get to know a bit about the biz by reading the finance section of *USA Today* or the *Wall Street Journal* for a few weeks. Then, make a short list of stocks you might want to buy and use the tools at MSN or Yahoo to research those companies.

• If you're saving for a more short-term goal, like a new bike or a computer, your best bet is high-yield savings or money market account or a CD. Be warned: a CD will tie up your money for a specific amount of time (six months to a year or more, depending on which plan you choose), so you need to evaluate the time frame – if you pull out early, you'll have to pay a fee.

KNOW THERE'S NO FREE MONEY:

• Credit cards are risky business and can get you in tons of trouble. Everything you charge needs to be paid back by the bill's due date – or you'll be charged – which can really add up. It's best to use cash or a debit card for everyday purchases.

• Be warned: Credit cards companies will record and report your action to a credit scoring company, who puts together a report on your debt and whether you pay your bills on time. If lenders don't like what they see on the report, you can be turned down for future credit cards, student loans— even insurance. Keep your record clean—and try to pay the bill off in full each month.

98. Make a *present* for your mom (or dad) at school. My mom always cries when I make her a gift. (Trust me, it's true)

Just 'cuz handprints and make-a-plates aren't on the curriculum anymore, doesn't mean your crafty gift-giving has to end. One of our fave DIY insiders is SANDRA MAGSAMEN, who besides writing a craft book, also created *Messages From The Heart*, a design brand of gifts and ideas to get folks (like us) to give with heart.

more

DIY Mother's Day (or any day) Gifts

1. Write a poem that shares how much you care. Make a list of the things you love about your mom. It only takes a few minutes to send a big message of appreciation and love.

2. Create a recipe book with your family's favorite dishes.

3. Frame a special letter, card, or poem that your mom wrote to you. If you are like me, I save everything and I have some really great poems, bits of wisdom, and expressions of love from mom. Frame one of your favorites in a nice frame for her. You'll be showing her that "because she said so" matters.

4. Make a book titled, You Are the Best Mother in the Universe. Ask sisters and brothers, even cousins and other relatives, to give you a list of the things they most respect, love, and admire about your mother. Fill the book with these thoughts and treasured photographs.

5. "Mom-nap" your mother and take her out for an adventure to a museum, an art gallery, a show, an outdoor garden... something she will love, and something that will surprise her.

HAYDEN PANETTIERE WITH MOM

Artful Father's Day (or any day) Gifts

NAKED BROTHERS BAND WITH DAD

1. Think of all the things your father likes and create the day around him. Type up an itinerary of the day's events for him to follow and tie a big bow on it!

2. Spend a day on the golf course with your dad if he likes to golf. Paint or glue little slips of paper with the words "I Love You," "You're the Greatest," or "Best Dad" on a set of golf balls as a gift (or tennis balls if that's his game).

3. Create a CD of your dad's favorite music. Design a cover for the CD case from a photograph you love or a special design you create. Be sure to put the year and date on the CD. Your dad will love to play it in the car or at work, and he will not only be singing to the tunes but will be singing your praises.

4. Gather up videotapes of different times in your life. Take them to the camera store where they will help you transfer them onto DVDs. You can decide how to organize the various films so that, in the end, you have one DVD that has many memories of the times you and your dad spent together. You can even get fancy and have music put in the background.

5. Really wash and dry your dad's car so it's shiny and bright and place a big bow on it with a note that reads "I love you," and I promise he will love you too for your effort.

99. Put together a favorite go-to outfit... something you know makes you look **super** cute!

Style is so much more than copying the latest looks in a mag or what your friends wear. Yes, we all know (or should know) there's more to life than trendy designer gear. But, dressing-up is a way to express yourself! Bloomingdale's fashion director STEPHANIE SOLOMON has some basic tips on different looks to go with different moods (and yes, we girls can be moody). No need to follow the rules exactly— just be inspired!

SPORTY

Fashion Icon: Vanessa Hudgens

Attitude: Comfy 'n Casual is your style 'tude. You need a cute outfit that compliments your active lifestyle. So, you can easily dash from class, to sports practice, to an after-school study session.

Go-To-Look: Hoodies, graphic t-shirts, jeans, and drawstring sweatpants are a few of your style basics. Wear your fave hoodie with a fitted message t-shirt (going green tees are super popular with celebs) underneath, and pair with dark-wash jeans. A boot-cut pair flatters all figure types, from curvy to petite. For a night out, swap the tee and hoodie with a bold-colored tunic over jeans.

Accents: Keep accessories to a minimum; a men's-style watch suits your sporty style and will help you keep track of your busy schedule. Converse or Vans sneaks are cool touches.

PREPPY

Fashion Icon: Taylor Momsen

Attitude: Practical 'n polished is your fashion sense. You prefer a look that matches your conservative nature and looks pulled-together, but doesn't scream look at me in the hallways.

Go-To-Look: Cardigans, pleated skirts, fitted Polos, khakis, and anything plaid are some of your wardrobe musts. You want traditional pieces that are easy to mix and match. Wear a solid-colored pleated skirt with a buttoned-up blouse. Add a pastel-colored cardigan and argyle kneesocks and you've got the Ivy League school spirit.

Accents: Headbands, ribbon belts or watchbands, stud earrings, loafers, and of course anything monogrammed are all classic preppy accessories.

GIRLY

Fashion Icon: Amanda Bynes

Attitude: Pretty in pink is your style instinct. You love to shop and hang with your girlfriends and want a look that matches your bubbly and super-fem personality.

Go-To-Look: Floral prints, ruffles, bows, or anything with lace are few of your fave things. Flaunt your girly sensibility with a flowy floral-print skirt and ruffled blouse. Top it off with a bright-colored cardigan cinched with a skinny belt to accentuate your girly waist.

Accents: Bow-tied ballerina flats or hair accessories, delicate drop-earrings, a cute clutch purse, and perfectly manicured nails are all girly essentials.

more

HIPSTER

Fashion Icon: Olsen Twins

Attitude: Bold 'n trendy is your clothes sense. You love attention-grabbing fashion, but NEVER copy the season's hottest styles. Instead, you crave a cutting-edge look that's all your own.

Go-To-Look: Vintage pieces, layered tees, girlie camis, long flowy skirts, leggings, and cropped blazers are a few of your fashion building blocks. A trendy pair of ankle boots worn tucked into skinny jeans or with a skirt can easily be dressed up or down.

Accents: Men's-inspired items like suspenders, ties, and fedoras can give a hipster spin to girlier pieces, like minis or skinny jeans. Chunky rings, layered necklaces, and an armful of bangles add funky touches.

100. Learn to **accept** a compliment.

We all love to hear nice things. So, why is it so tough to simply smile and say thanks to our admirers? Somebody says "great tennis match" or "those jeans look fab" —we spill but... "My butt is huge" or "My serve sucks." **JESS WEINER** (aka the queen of self-esteem) leads workshops to help young gals build up their self-love.

more

JESS'S TIPS TO HELP YOU LOVE YOURSELF!

Be silly. Silly people have more fun and laughter is good for you.

Be a good listener. You'll learn a lot about yourself when you listen to others.

Be a good loser. Don't be afraid of messing up or failing—that's how we learn to do things better.

Be a gracious winner. Enjoy being #1 but remember not to rub it in anyone's face.

Be emotional. Yes, emotions are good things—cry, scream, laugh, yell—it's all normal and good to get it out.

Be kind. Never underestimate how much a smile can lift someone's day. Doing nice things for people makes you feel good.

Be honest. Try to speak what's in your heart—even when it's difficult. When we are honest we feel more powerful.

"Giving up is not part of my vocabulary. Sure, I get down, but I've learned to let the negative roll off my back. You have to if you want to keep on going in this world."

–Jordin

FEEL-GOOD SITES:

There're lots of girls who feel just like you. ...Click on these girl-power sites to empower YOU!

www.girlslife.com

www.girlsinc.org

www.beinggirl.com

www.studio2b.org

101. Have a major *pillow fight* with your best buds or siblings.

hotlist **13** must-know events in American History

1. **American Revolutionary War:** Wahoo! Cut the cord from England and won the freedom to build our own rockin' country.

2. **Bill of Rights:** Without these basic freedoms of speech, religion, and the right to a fair trial—let's just say reading a book, watching TV, or going to worship would be a totally different experience.

3. **Civil War:** What's up with our ancestors? Hard to believe our country was split in two—North and South—and some folks were cool with that.

4. **Segregation:** Can you imagine not being able to hang with your buds just because they were a different race? Thankfully most of that nasty hate ended with the Civil Rights Act of 1964, which banned segregation.

5. **19th Amendment:** Shocking that we powerful gals couldn't vote until 1920. We've come a long way, baby! Today a woman has run for the Oval Office and I'm sure a female will be sitting pretty as Prez soon.

6. **Great Depression:** Let's just say America went into major debt and paying the bills wasn't easy.

7. **Holocaust:** A sad chapter in history. Hilter declared a massive campaign of hate against Jews and killed over 6 million people, simply because they were different.

8. **Atomic Bomb:** The U.S. dropped the atomic bomb on Japan. The U.S. declared victory, but many saw the bombing as extreme bullying. This was the first (and hopefully the last) use of the atomic bomb.

9. **Cold War:** The longest war in our history involved not weapons but egos. The U.S. wanted to stop the spread of communism. The 35-year-old chill defrosted with the collapse of communism in 1990.

10. **First Man on The Moon:** One small step for man, one giant leap for mankind! A major adventure into space that showed the world just how sweet advances in science and technology really are! (And it would be HUMANkind, today!)

11. **9/11/01:** The Twin Towers in New York City and the Pentagon in D.C. were attacked by terrorists who had hijacked jets. Many people lost their lives, and we were around to see it go down. We should all try to take something positive away from the experience and be more compassionate.

12. **Iraq War:** This war started because Americans were led to believe that Iraq could harm us, and there is tons of controversy surrounding why our country really went to war. As of the writing of this book, this war is still going on. I hope our troops come safely home soon.

13. On December 14, 1994, at 7:36pm Brittany Marie MacLeod was born into this fab world and has been shaking it up ever since.

"Plymouth Plantation in Massachusetts, where they re-create the Mayflower, was my favorite place to visit. I love history. So, for all 13-year-olds, learn a piece of history. It is wicked cool."

— JoJo

103. Shine like a star with **glitter**.

Sparkle like a star! Hilary Duff loves to make her eyes pop with a glittery silver liner. And our favorite supermodels (like Gisele and Heidi Klum) know shimmer rules on the runway. Victoria's Secret **LINDA HAY** has the DIY tips on glitter.

Product: Glitter shadow, try Victoria's Secret Silky Eye Shadow. Eye Liner, try Victoria's Secret Sparkling Eye Liner.

Cheeks: Dust a little glitter to the tops of the cheekbones. It will give more extreme contour to your facial structure. Try Victoria's Secret Mosaic Blush.

Eyes: Do either a glitter shadow or liner—never both. If using a glitter shadow only apply to eyelid. With a liner, a simple line on your top lash is all you need.

Body: Dust glitter all over the body with a large powder brush. Brush a line down the front and back of legs, from the thigh to the toes. Also do a line down the arms and across the collar. Have fun with it but beware of overdoing it. Less is more with glitter!

104. Don't fight with your sibs for an **entire** week (tough, right?).

Hanging with your bro or sis is right in style! The Jonas Brothers, the Duff sisters, and the Williams sisters are often spotted together—and show there's no stronger bond than family. Teen superstar **BRENDA SONG** says her favorite role off-camera is as a big sis. The *Zack & Cody* star admits her two bros can be annoying (hey, isn't that what bros do?), but there's nobody she trusts more.

BRENDA'S SIB SURVIVAL RULES!

SIBS ARE BUILT-IN FRIENDS FOR LIFE:

• Friends come & go, but your family is with your 4ever, so why not get along? Even though I am the oldest, my two brothers are my protectors. They're always there to defend me or simply listen to my problems (and not tell my secrets).

Supermodel, sister, and mother of two, Veronica Webb shared 5 fave things all sibs can do together. Don't have one? Me neither—and lots of my buds don't either. So, recruit a fellow onesie and L.H.L.A.S. (love-her-like-a-sister).

1. Switch lives for a day! Walk, talk, and dress like your sibling or best friend. Do all the great things they do and make fun of all the annoying things they do.

2. Save up for something big together. Do you dream of going to Paris? Taking horseback riding lessons? Surf camp? You name it. Make a business plan with your sib and stick to it.

3. Write a song about someone in your family. I guarantee you no one will ever forget such a thoughtful a gift. I'd say it's the coolest present ever!

4. Get a video camera and/or a scrapbook, and put together a family history. You'd be surprised how interesting it is to get friends and family talking about "the olden days." Hearing tales of what your family did back in the days before cell phones, ATMs, and the internet might just blow your mind.

5. Make portraits of each other. Sign and date them with the year. On the back write 10 things you think your sibling or best friend will be doing at the age of 30.

SISTERS VENUS AND SERENA

SPEND TIME TOGETHER; JUST YOU AND YOUR SIBS.

• Whether it's playing video games, going out to dinner, or hanging in the park, get to know each other. Sounds dorky, but my 12-year-old brother and I love to cook. We chop veggies and swap stories about our day. It's an awesome way to chill. My 18-year-old brother is my best workout bud.

FIGHT FAIR:

• I've caught my brothers snooping through my diary and listening in on my phone convos—so not cool! But instead of a crazy blowups, we write letters. Putting our anger/hurt down on paper lets each other know exactly how we're feeling. As we get older, our letters get shorter, because we're better able to express ourselves without name-calling.

105. Personalize your shoes, a tshirt, jeans—something! (Make it scream you!)

DIY DECORATIONS

Glittered Necklace T-shirt

Designed by Cheryl Ball, courtesy of www.tulipfashionart.com

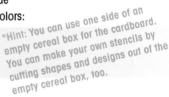

MATERIALS NEEDED

- Black t-shirt
- Cardboard for shirt*
- White chalk
- Pots of different sizes (optional)
- Tulip® Sticky Fabric Stencils™ or cardboard for making your own stencils (think Xs, circles, equal signs, hearts, or charms.)
- Scissors
- Small paintbrush
- Tulip® Fashion Glitter Bond™ or fabric glue
- Tulip® Fashion Glitter™ in the following colors:
  Silver, Gold, Pink, Red,
  Turquoise, Royal blue
- Scratch paper
- A glass, jar, or can (optional)

*Hint: You can use one side of an empty cereal box for the cardboard. You can make your own stencils by cutting shapes and designs out of the empty cereal box, too.

INSTRUCTIONS:

For best results, please read all instructions before beginning project. Refer to photo for color and design placement.

1. Prewash your t-shirt. Don't use fabric softener, though! Then place a piece of cardboard inside the shirt so that paint won't seep through.

3. Use the white chalk to lightly draw half circles that follow the neckline of your shirt. These are the outlines of the necklaces. You might trace the bottom of three different sized pots or pans to make the half circle precise.

4. Create the stencils for the necklace links from the cardboard or use the stencils you already have at home (stencils with charms work great). We suggest an X, which can be made by cutting a plus sign and turning it sideways, a zero or circle, an equal sign, and a heart.

5. For each link of each necklace, place the stencil along your chalked necklace line, dip brush into glue or glitter bond, then carefully brush into stencil and onto the black t-shirt, applying a thin even coat and being sure not to go past outside edges of the stencil. Immediately pour glitter into stencil. We suggest you use silver glitter for the X, gold glitter for the circles, silver glitter for the equal sign, pink glitter for the hearts, and then go crazy with your charm stencils!

6. Use your finger to lightly press glitter into adhesive.

7. Shake excess glitter onto scratch paper – this can be reused later.

8. Carefully peel off stencil.

9. Repeat steps working up both sides of neckline.

10. Repeat steps for remaining chains of necklace.

11. If you'd like, you can repeat these steps on one sleeve. Insert a glass, jar, or can inside the sleeve to keep paint from seeping through.

12. Let dry, and wear it loud and proud!

Phone Number Sneakers

Designed by Suzie Shinseki, courtesy of www.tulipfashionart.com

MATERIALS NEEDED:

Pair of white sneakers with laces

- Tulip® Soft Fabric Paint™ in the following colors:
  Yellow, Royal Blue, Red, Black
- Foil, approximately 10 x 10"
- Sponge
- Plastic container for water
- Painter's tape
- 1" brush

- Glossy Instant Decoupage (we suggest Aleene's® Collage Pauge Instant Decoupage)
- Old phonebook yellow pages torn into various size pieces
- Tulip® Spirit™ Fabric Markers in the following colors:
  Blue, Red, Black
- Old toothbrush

more

INSTRUCTIONS:

For best results, please read all instructions before beginning project. Refer to photo for color and design placement.

1. Remove laces from shoes.

2. Pour small puddles of yellow, red, and royal blue fabric paint, spaced about 2" apart, on the piece of foil.

3. Lay shoelaces flat on newspaper. Dip sponge into yellow paint and apply paint ¼ of the way down from one end, covering both sides. Rinse sponge and dip into red paint. Apply red paint to shoelace, beginning right below the yellow and applying another ¼ of the way on both sides. Repeat with the royal blue paint. Then put the laces aside to dry.

4. Run painter's tape along the bottom rubber and rubber toe areas of the sneaker to protect them. Also tape area where shoe tongue is exposed.

5. Using the brush, apply instant decoupage on areas of the shoe to be covered with paper, working in small sections. Immediately apply instant decoupage to torn yellow page pieces and place on already decoupaged portion of shoe. Cover the paper and shoe with an additional layer of instant decoupage. Continue in this fashion until the entire shoe is covered with the exception of the taped areas. Allow to dry.

6. Using the fabric marker pens, write names of friends and their phone numbers all over the shoes.

7. Pour small puddle of black paint on foil and dilute with a small amount of water.

8. Place toothbrush bristles into the paint and using your index finger, pull bristles back to spatter over the shoe. Spatter as much or as little as you wish. Allow to dry.

For more fabulous craft ideas, visit
www.tulipfashionart.com *and* **www.duncancrafts.com**

106. Make ice cream out of snow!

RECIPE FOR ICE CREAM SNOW

- 1 gallon snow
- 3/4 cup white sugar
- 1 tablespoon vanilla extract
- 2 cups milk (or less)

When it starts to snow, place a large, clean bowl outside to collect the flakes. When full, stir in sugar and vanilla to taste, then stir in just enough milk for the desired consistency.

Just like your first party dress or pair of fancy shoes, a purse is a rite of passage. A sign we're ready to lose the Dora-the-Explorer backpack and lug our stuff in something a bit more grown-up. Fashion gal **ALYSON DEYETTE** offers the 4-1-1 on how to mix and match your personality with the bag you carry.

Messenger Bag: Perfect for the cool and laid-back Bohemian. Worn slung across her body, she's hands-free to dash from class to meeting up with friends after school.

Shoulder Bag: A future stylista. This bold gal wants to show off her fashion 'tude with a flashy bag. She's ready to be independent and carry it all, and knows how to flaunt a go-get' em confidence.

Organic Tote: No leather for this eco-conscious gal. This green-eyed shopper wants to make a 'save the planet' statement with her comfy tote.

Backpack: Right on for the active gal, who needs to carry both her books and sports jersey. It combines your competitive need-to-win spirit with your no-nonsense style.

Clutch: This diva-in-training doesn't want her bag to outshine her fab outfit. All she needs in her itty purse is a lip gloss and her cell. She'll get someone else to carry her books.

Hint: Don't spend major cash on a trendy purse. There are lots of affordable (and cool) brands, just right for teens.

Cheap 'n Chic Purse Brands:
Lucky Brand
Baby Phat
Tommy Hilfiger
Guess
XOXO
American Eagle
Kipling
JanSport
LeSportsac
Roxy

CLUTCH

SHOULDER BAG

108. Rake the leaves, make a gigantic pile, and **jump in**. (Not too many times: as this move will upset your parents and you'll risk your allowance.)

109. Give A *Speech*

If oral reports make your stomach turn and your voice crack—ITS NOT JUST YOU! Public speaking is many peeps' number one fear. Speaking pro JILL ESPLIN works with teens to get over their fears and go for their dreams. "'Confidence comes with competence.' I heard this quote when I first started speaking and I was told to PRACTICE, PRACTICE, PRACTICE! This is true for many things in life and especially with public speaking."

Hello!

SPEAK LIKE A PRO!

- Brainstorm and write out your speech word for word. Then review it and make the changes that will spice it up and make it memorable for the audience.

- Involve the audience. You can ask a question, get a volunteer, or have them imagine something in their mind's eye. Give them an experience, not just a bunch of words.

- Always do a "dress rehearsal" or a full run through of your speech. Stand up and actually deliver your speech as if a real audience was watching you.

- Tape record yourself and notice your "buzz words" such as... ahhh, like, um, so and, ok, etc. Once you know them, avoid them and use the power of the pause.

- Have fun and remember the audience wants you to do well. They are not looking for your flaws.

STOP THE DRAMA!

Who doesn't love a juicy bit of gossip? I am wa-y-y-y into teen mags and all the scoop on my favorite celebs. But, dishing on your buds is not cool. I know. I know. It's hard to resist listening to and then passing on the latest "did you hear what so and so did." But before you do—think—would you want the same said about you? Gossip hurts feelings—reputations—and is no way to build a sisterhood. *Gossip Girl's* **KELLY RUTHERFORD** stars as Blake Lively's mom. While the show can get downright catty—the actress shares why we should all live in a gossip-free zone!

• Words are very powerful. Make yours positive. The next time a friends starts to gossip about someone else, just smile. You don't have to add your 2 cents.

• Gossips are often insecure. They put down others to reinforce their own social status. Make yourself feel better by avoiding talking trash.

• Be grateful for your friends. Friendship is a gift. Don't treat it poorly by spreading rumors.

• Gossip is often aimed at someone we are envious of. Instead of bringing them down, be inspired.

• Be kind to the person being talked about. Building up other people's confidence will also make yours stronger.

• Remember: The less you gossip, the less people will gossip about you.

PERK UP

DANITY KANE'S **SHANNON BEX** SHARES THE SIMPLE THINGS IN LIFE THAT ALWAYS MAKE HER SMILE.

SPENDING TIME OUTDOORS:
- I am from Oregon, so there's nothing like a crisp fall day. I love to get cozy in my favorite sweater, sip some cocoa, and a take a deep breath of autumn air.

ANIMALS:
- I love my doggies. Just watching them play makes me happy. Also, I love to be around horses; they are such amazing beautiful creatures. I could sit and watch them for hours.

MUSIC:
- Country music makes my heart happy. Play a little Garth Brooks and I'm a happy camper.
- Dancing and singing are two of my greatest joys. It doesn't have to be on a stage in front of a huge audience. Some of my best dancing and singing moments are in my room by myself.

CHURCH:
- Simply because it centers me.

MY FAVORITE FOODS:
- My husband is awesome at bringing home my favorite goodies when I'm having a bad day or not feeling well. Nothing's yummier than a grocery bag stuffed with black olives, raspberries, blackberries, or strawberries, sweet chocolate, and chicken noodle soup.

MY FAMILY:
- I have a very close and open relationship with my family. I love that I can call my mom, my brother, or my dad and talk about anything, vent, or ask an odd question. From "mom how long are eggs good after the expiration date?" or "dad, what type of countertop would you suggest, granite or concrete?"
- I feel truly blessed for all the wonderful people in my life!

112. Read this book **again.**

113. *Love* your family and friends, and tell them often how much you care.

A big smack-a-roo to all the celebs who generously contributed their heart-felt expertise!

- J. Alexander
- Criss Angel
- Shannon Bex
- Sabrina Bryan
- Billy Bush
- Brandi Chastain
- Clique Girlz
- Tabitha & Napoleon D'Umo
- Tiffany Giardina
- Selena Gomez
- Ashley Greene
- Katie Lee Joel
- Matt Lauer
- Kimora Lee
- Rachelle Lefevre
- Meaghan Jette Martin
- Maria Menounos
- Kellie Pickler
- Nancy O'Dell
- Kelly Rutherford
- Brenda Song
- Alyson Stoner
- Taylor Swift
- Cast of *13 The Musical*
- Veronica Webb

A kiss to all our Special Peeps:

First off, major props to Judy Linden, Katie Feiereisel, and the Stonesong Press crew, who guided this book from the very beginning. Thanks to Harlequin and our editor Deborah Brody for making this little book of girl power a big dream come true. A lot of hard work went into this—but it's totally worth it and dedicated to all the fab tweenagers out there!

Thanks to our awesome supporters: The *Access Hollywood* team; the best group of co-workers ever! Chad Bergacs, Jeneine Doucette, Christine Fahey, Nancy Harrison, Nomi Pincus, Jen Zweben, The NYC Access crews (the most amazing buds & supporters), Rob Silverstein, and Claudia Eaton.

Most of all, a big sa-weet kiss to our family and friends; especially Lois & John MacLeod and Aunt Lesley—you've been our greatest champions!

A major shout-out to our fab Girl-Power contributors:

...THE EXPERTS ARE THE HEART OF THIS BOOK:

AllyKatzz is a super-cool 100 percent monitored social networking site for girls age 10–15, founded by tween expert Denise Restauri. Denise generously got her gang onboard and provided invaluable real tween insight. Learn more about Denise and the AllyKatzz gang at www.allykatzz.com.

American Camping Association is a go-to site for children and adults. Its goal is to preserve and promote the camp experience. There are over 2,400 ACA-accredited camps that meet up to 300 health and safety standards. For more information visit www.CampParents.org.

Michelle Barge is a NYC yoga instructor and a good friend who shared her zen insight on yoga for teens. She also teaches yoga to NYC high school students and is the eco-living expert for www.beyoumag.com.

Lew Beyer is an etiquette expert with www.civilityexperts.com.

Debi Byrnes is the founder of Clear Up Skincare, which provides an educational outreach program to middle and high school students about the physical and emotional effects of acne. Learn more at www.clearupskincare.org.

Jean Chatzky is an award-winning journalist, best-selling author, and well-respected finance expert. Among her many credits, she's the financial editor for NBC's *Today* and a contributor to the *Oprah Winfrey Show*.

Chris Colbeck is a 20-year veteran of the fashion biz. The English-born makeup artist travels the world working on magazine spreads and with celebrities. He makes his home in New York City and is represented by Art Department.

Debra Martin Chase is Hollywood's Queen of Tweens. Her company Martin Chase Productions is an affiliate of the Walt Disney Company. She's produced amazing movie series, such as *The Cheetah Girls*, *The Sisterhood of the Traveling Pants*, and *The Princess Diaries*.

Rebecca Cole is a New York City garden, floral, and interior designer. She is the founder of Cole Creates, a retail and design business.

Dashing Diva is a luxe nail spa with locations worldwide. These nail gurus also provide a full line of products. Check them out at www.dashingdiva.com.

Alison Deyette is a seasoned stylist and lifestyle expert and a go-to fashion source for national news and entertainment programs, magazines, and online media outlets. Check out her Web site at www.alionthego.com.

Julia DeVillers is a well-known advocate of girl power and author of *Girlwise: How to Be Confident, Capable, Cool, and In Control.* She's also teamed up with Cheetah Girl Sabrina Bryan to co-author *Princess of Gossip.*

Danielle Getty is a registered dietician/nutritionist for Joy Bauer Nutrition, New York.

Dosomething.org is an awesome Web site for teens who are interested in volunteering, learning about different causes, and taking action to make the world a better place. Check it out at www.dosomething.org.

Jill Esplin speaks, writes, and facilitates student programs worldwide that inspire young people to make a difference in their lives and others. Find out more on Jill and her self-leadership message at www.leadingforlife.com.

Mandy Forr is senior editor at *Girls' Life* magazine. She's got all deets on everything tween and shares juicy tidbits on LIFE with young girls in their monthly mag and on their fab site, www.girlslife.com.

Girlstart is a nonprofit organization founded in Austin, Texas, created to empower girls to excel in math, science, and technology. Find out more at www.girlstart.org.

Katie & Melissa Havard are a mother-daughter duo who write about teen issues for an advice column on www.lovetoknow.com and www.hangproud.com.

Kiss is a one-stop shop for handy helpers, from nail colors to mani-pedi kits to cool decals. Check it out at www.kissusa.com.

KIDPOWER International™ is a charitable educational organization. KIDPOWER teaches people of different ages and abilities to be successful in learning and practicing personal safety, self-protection, confidence, and advocacy skills. See their Web site for more information: www.kidpower.org.

Linda Hay, makeup artist, and **Alison Greenberg,** publicist, shared the secrets of Victoria's Secret beauty with *113 Things To Do By 13.* Thanks for your massive support from the get-go! See www.victoriassecret.com/beauty for more.

Mary Jennings is New York City–based singer and songwriter. To learn more, see www.myspace.com/jenningsmusic.

Jennifer Kushell is the co-founder of www.YSN.com—your success network—the leading network of young entrepreneurs in over 100 countries. Jennifer is also the *New York Times* best-selling author of *Secrets of the Young & Successful.*

Sandra Magsamen is an artist, art therapist, mom, award-winning author of *Living Artfully,* and the creator of the Messages from the Heart brand. Learn more about Sandra and her amazing crafts at www.sandramagsamen.com.

New Moon Media was an invaluable source for rounding up insightful real girl voices on issues such as leadership and OMG moments. Girls ages 8–12 can enjoy the magazine, *New Moon Girls* and the New Moon Girls on-line community. Both are fab reads and blog sites for young teens. Check it out at www.newmoon.org.

Dawn Nocera is a nationally recognized life coach and creator of www.educatingjane.com, a Web site whose mission is to educate, motive, and inspire girls and young women to reach their dreams and beyond.

Meaghan O'Neil is a green guru as the editor of eco-sites www.treehugger.com and www.planetgreen.com. She's also the co-author of *Ready, Set, Green: Eight Weeks to Modern Eco-living.*

Oceana is a New York City-based yoga teacher. She is also a holistic health counselor. Learn more: www.oceanayoga.com.

Prudential Spirit of Community Awards honors young people in middle and high school for outstanding volunteer service to their communities. Applications forms for the awards are available at local schools, Girl Scout councils, and county 4-H offices throughout the U.S. Or, interested students can visit www.prudential.com/community/spirit.

Dominic Pucciarello is New York City–based hairstylist. He's the go-to guy for Victoria's Secret models Adriana Lima and Marisa Miller.

Jose Rivera is the lead makeup artist for Sephora pro beauty team. He teaches the Sephora team the latest makeup tips and tricks. Click onto the hottest makeup trends and products at www.sephora.com.

Sharon Scott is a Frisco, Texas, based family counselor and conducts workshops on her Peer Pressure Reveral program (www.sharonscott.com). She's the author of 9 books, including her teen guide, *How to Say No and Keep Your Friends, 2nd Edition*.

Witt Siasoco is the Teen Programs Manager at the Walker Arts Center in Minneapolis and runs the Walker Arts Center Teen Arts Council.

Dr. Robyn Silverman's pioneering work with young women has established her as a body image expert in academia, the national media, and among parents and their daughters. As a way to interact with girls personally, Dr. Silverman created *The Sassy Sisterhood Girls Circle*, a program for preadolescent girls that explores issues that affect body esteem and self-image. Learn more at her Web site, www.drrobynsblog.com.

A big thanks to Lori Singer, V.P. Global Marketing Coty Prestige Designer Fragrances & Alana Wodnicki, Public Relations Coty, for providing a whiff of scents-ability.

A big shout-out to Bloomingdale's Stephanie Solomon, V.P. of Fashion and Elizabeth Quarta, director of Public Relations, who both generously shared their style expertise.

Genevieve Thiers is the founder and CEO of www.sittercity.com. With more than 150 thousand caregivers across the country, Sittercity is the nation's largest database for nannies, babysitters, and pet sitters. Check out their Web site at www.sittercity.com.

David Tutera is a celebrity party planner. He's planned bashes for Jennifer Lopez, Matthew McConaughey, the Rolling Stones, plus many more. He's the author of 4 books, including *Big Birthdays*.

Alyson Udell and Duncan Crafts, thanks for creating the fabulous DIY Crafts. Get lots of crafty inspiration at www.duncancrafts.com.

Jessica Weiner is an author, self-esteem expert, and advice columnist, committed to transforming the self-esteem of women and girls worldwide. Jess is the global ambassador for the Dove Self-Esteem Fund.

Dawn Windsor is the founder of Windsor Virtual Office Solutions and has the 4-1-1 on organization. Learn more at www.windsorvos.com.

Kelly White is managing editor of girlworlddaily.com, an internationally syndicated online magazine for teens and 'tweens.

credits